SCOTLAND'S
FORgotten
VALOUR

D1421889

by Graham Ross

This book is dedicated to my family past and present
who have put up with my obsessive interest in the
'Victoria Cross'.

ISBN   1899272 00 3

MacLean Press, 60 Aird Bhearnasdail, by Portree, Isle of Skye Tel:0470 532 309

Cover: *Sgt Major William Robertson of the 'Gordon Highlanders winning his VC at Elandslaagte, South Africa, 21 October 1899.*

CONTENTS

Bill Reid V.C. with Iain Nicolson D.F.C. D.F.M.

FOREWORD

I am indeed honoured to have been asked to give this forward to "Scotland's FORgotten VALOUR".

Because of the formation of the Victoria Cross and George Cross Association after the last war, I had the privilege and opportunity, to meet and talk with, all the Scottish holders over the years. As you can expect, they were all unassuming "heroes", who felt privileged to have been awarded the highest of honours, and made little fuss of the actions which had prompted the award.

I remember in my own case, the night I was in the convalescent ward at R.A.F. Ely Hospital, when I had a telephone call from our Air Officer Commanding, A.V.M. Cochrane. He told me that "The King had been graciously pleased to award you the Victoria Cross" ' I almost fainted. To me ' it was like getting 100% in English at school ' which I hadn't long left.

Over the years, I have been asked, what it feels like to have been awarded the Victoria Cross. If I can use my own action to explain my feelings.

When we were flying back home from the raid, over the Channel that night, the four engines cut out. It seemed, that as the Flight Engineer had been so involved with helping me keep the aircraft flying correctly, we had forgotten to switch the petrol tanks to maintain level fuel after the target. When the engines stopped ' he remembered this and switched over the tanks ' the engines restarting and we proceeded towards the English Coast.

Had we crashed into the sea ' no one would have known any better and our story would never have been told. I refer to this, as we had in effect completed the action, for which the Victoria Cross was awarded, other than land the plane.

How many times, must something similar have happened to crews on operations, soldiers and sailors in action ' with no one to tell their story.

My answer to how I feel is that it is worn with those in mind, who carried out their duties, but were unable to tell their story.

This is a book which epitomises the debt of gratitude to those who fought, those who suffered and above all those who made the ultimate sacrifice, that succeeding generations might live in freedom.

Their memory is immortal!

William "Bill" Reid V.C.,B.Sc
Crieff
January 1994

PREFACE

"Soldiers of the 42nd, 79th and 93rd, Old Highland Brigade with whom I have passed the early and perilous part of this war, I now have to take leave of you. In a few hours I shall be on board ship never to see you again as a body, a long farewell. I am now old and shall not be called to serve any more, and nothing will remain with me but the memory of my campaign and the enduring, hardy, generous soldiers with whom I have been associated, whose name and glory will long be kept in the hearts of our countrymen. When you go home as you gradually fulfil your term of service, each to his family and cottage, you will tell the story of your immortal advance in that victorious echelon up the heights of the Alma and of the old Brigadier who led you and loved you so well. Your children and your childrens' children will repeat the tale to other generations when only a few lines of history will remain to record all the enthusiasm and discipline which have borne you so stoutly to the end of this war. Our native land will never forget the name of the Highland Brigade and in some future war that native land will call for another one to equal this, which it can never surpass. Though I shall be gone, the thought of you will go with me wherever I may be and cheer my old age with a glorious recollection of danger confronted and hardships endured. A pipe will never sound near me without carrying me back to those bright days when I was at your head and wore the bonnet which you gained for me and the honourable decorations on my breast, many of which I owe to your conduct. Brave soldiers, kind comrades, farewell."

[The farewell speech of Sir Colin Campbell to the men of the Highland Brigade (Crimea 1855)].

The birth of this book took place in the late 1960's when as a young man wishing to impress a new girl friend I would spend many lunch breaks from my employment with Glasgow Corporation at the Mitchell Library in Glasgow writing out the citations from the London Gazette for the men who had won the Victoria Cross. In later years when the family had grown up or at least did not need the guidance of their father I was able to resurrect my study of the Victoria Cross. (A subject which is best discussed amongst parties having a little knowledge). I rapidly found out that my generation, born after the last great increase in Victoria Cross heroes, World War Two, were not aware of any of these men. They have to all intents and purposes been forgotten. It is often said that old soldiers do not die they just fade away and this is certainly the case as far as our nations Victoria Cross winners are concerned.

In the 1960's it was still possible to meet a few of these men and ask them to describe how they had won the country's highest decoration for bravery. They were still afforded a position of honour at the annual Armistice Day parades held throughout the land (albeit in fewer numbers as years went by). Today there is only a total of 34 alive in the World and only 2 in Scotland. In order to prove my point I carried out a small survey to find out the extent of various peoples knowledge of Victoria Cross winners and more especially those winners whose place of birth was Scotland. To my disappointment the younger generation were totally ignorant on the subject and almost to a man and certainly a woman none could name any Scots born winners. The generation in the 60+ age bracket could still remember a few names and again in the survey only 2 men, both 65+, could name one winner born in Scotland.

As a result this book begun almost 30 years ago had to be resurrected in order to try and redress the balance of knowledge of these men who in any other country of the world would have the status of nothing less than "Heroes" of their country instead of being Scotland's Forgotten Valour.

Isle of Skye, October 1993

ACKNOWLEDGEMENTS

It would have been impossible to write this book without the help and support of my many friends and relatives. Firstly the patience of my wife Elspeth and family, for putting up with my disappearing on a nightly basis to the "computer room" to play with the family word processor. (She must however admit to part of the blame because she had taken the time to teach me the rudiments of this piece of modern technology).

Secondly, my family Colin, Morag and Neil who have suffered by not being the beneficiaries of my discipline for long periods of time. It had to be said that latterly it was not uncommon for me to be banished to the "computer room" to get me out of the road.

Special mention must go to Major Haig MacDonald M.C., of Drumnadrochit for the information and research on his local Victoria Cross winner, Private Roderick McGregor which was of immense value as my own research progressed. At the same time I am indebted to Geoff Robertson, a friend to many VC winners, including Bill Reid, who was of immense help and encouragement in getting this book onto paper.

Further mention of a general nature must be made of the various Museums and Regimental Headquarters who helped to confirm information I had gathered about their own Victoria Cross winners.

The following people also deserve special mention:'

Bill Reid VC BSc, John A Cruickshank VC, Reg King, Lady Patricia Miers, Miss Margaret Gallagher, Ian MacLeod, Di Alexander, Peter Fulton, Ian Nicolson DFC DFM, Major William Shaw MBE, Betty Luke, Henry Freckleton, Vice Admiral Sir Roderick MacDonald KBE, Sandra MacDonald, Jimmy Gibson, David Bisset, Bob Young, Alex Hill, Neil Gerrard, Iain Smith.

I would like to mention all who, over the years, have helped me gather information about the Victoria Cross and who must have wondered where it was all going to lead to.

I would like to thank the following for permission to reproduce the illustrations used in the text.

The Royal Archives © HM The Queen (*fig 5*)
Moray District Council (*fig 2*)
Argyll & Sutherland Highlanders Museum (*figs 3, 4, 13, 16*)
The Black Watch Museum (*figs 6,9*)
Hamilton District Council (*fig 7*)
The Royal Scots Museum (*figs 10, 15*)
Henry Freckleton (*fig 11*)
K.O.S.B. Museum (*figs 12, 17*)
Dingwall Museum (*fig 14*)
Imperial War Museum (*figs 18, 19, 20, 21, 23, 24, 25, 28, 29*)
Lady Patricia Miers (*fig 22*)
William Reid VC (*fig 26*)
John A. Cruickshank VC (*fig 27*)
D.C. Thomson & Co. Ltd (*fig 40*)
Thames Television Ltd. (*fig 42*)

INTRODUCTION

In June 1991 the list of decorations awarded for the Gulf War was published and to the surprise of many there was no award of the Victoria Cross. In spite of the fact that several papers had carried the story of a Posthumous Victoria Cross to a soldier of the Special Air Service for activities behind enemy lines. Much was made of the fact that this soldier was to be named, in direct contradiction to the policy on awards and decorations to the members of the British Special Forces.

There was however an award of a Posthumous Military Medal to Corporal Denbury of the Special Air Service who had been killed whilst operating behind Iraqi lines. One would wonder if he was originally recommended for the Victoria Cross and this was reduced to the Military Medal. This should not be construed as a diminution on the Corporals conduct but as an indication of the way in which the action which would merit an award of the Victoria Cross has become more difficult to achieve as our Armed Services become more efficient and highly trained. There is no doubt that many early awards would by todays standards have resulted in the award of a Military Medal or even Mentioned in Despatches. It is to the eternal credit of the powers who make the final decision on an award that they have striven to maintain the highest standards in gallantry, and not been influenced by the ever present media in this modern world.

All too often nowadays our heroes do not get the public recognition which they rightly deserve especially in this world of immediate media involvement. This can be testified by the length of memory for the Gulf War awards.

This contrasts greatly to the first awards of the Victoria Cross which were reported widely in the press both locally and nationally and these recipients remained for the most part heroes throughout their lives. Many officers winning the Victoria Cross went on to the top in their military career. This is certainly the case of Lieutenant F S Roberts who won his Cross during the Indian Mutiny and remained a hero throughout his life until his death in November 1914 as Field Marshal "Bobs" V.C. As he died many more were to join the ranks of heroes and "Bobs" faded from the memory of all but a few.

These First World War heroes were the earliest recollection I have of the existence of Victoria Cross heroes. I remember vividly seeing several old men on the platform for the march past at the Cenotaph in George Square, Glasgow at the annual Armistice ceremonies. Among these was Driver Fred Luke, Royal Field Artillery, who was one of the first to be awarded the Victoria Cross in 1914 about the same time as Field Marshal Roberts died. This elderly group soon disappeared over what seemed like a few years. As I stood there watching the even less known bemedalled heroes I remember asking my father about the Victoria Cross. To my young mind he seemed knowledgeable and did in fact have a Victoria Cross connection, in that during his service in the Western Desert the unit in which he was serving was able to pick up the survivors from the raid on Rommell's headquarters at Beda Littoria, Libya. This raid resulted in the award of a Posthumous Victoria Cross to Scots born Lieutenant Colonel Geoffrey Keyes of the Royal Scots Greys. He also worked with another Scot, Private Jimmy Stokes, serving with the Kings Shropshire Light Infantry, who won a Posthumous Victoria Cross at Kervenheim, Rhineland on the 1 March 1945. Later on when I went to Secondary School I realised that my school, Shawlands Academy, had its very own Victoria Cross hero in the shape of Lieutenant Donald Cameron, Royal Navy, who won his Victoria Cross against the German battleship "Tirpitz". Glasgow over the years has certainly had its fair share of Victoria Cross heroes of which very few are remembered outside their immediate family.

The award of the Victoria Cross has not in many cases resulted in instant fame or fortune. Some Victoria Cross heroes have had to take advantage of the fact that they held the Cross to earn a living as the monetary gains attached to the award were and still are practically nil. Piper Findlater, serving with the Gordon Highlanders, won his award for distinguished gallantry at the storming of the Dargai Heights, Afghanistan in 1897. After recuperating from his wounds, received in the action, he was prominent in piping circles, where, with the scars from his wounds still visible above his hose, he made his living playing his pipes at local ceilidhs. In spite of this a national hero having to play in Music Halls throughout the country the annual pension attached to the award was not increased from £10 to its present level of £100 per annum until 1959 when it was increased in response to a question by Jackie Smyth VC in the House of Commons.

In more recent times Sergeant John Hannah from Paisley, serving in the Royal Air Force, and in fact the youngest Victoria Cross winner of the Second World War having been invalided out of the service as a result of burns received whilst winning his Victoria Cross had to go round Music Halls in wartime Britain recalling how he had won his medal. This was seen as a boost to morale in times when all was not going to Britains advantage. Another winner who used his experiences well was Frogman VC Lieutenant Ian Fraser of the Royal Naval Reserve, by setting up a successful diving company. This contrasts with the other Victoria Cross winner who was with Lieutenant Fraser in the Johore Straits on 31 July 1945, James Magennis. He was forced to sell his medal in 1952 for the princely sum of £75.

There is at least one example of the award of the Victoria Cross possibly costing the recipient money. Inverness born Colour Sergeant Henry MacDonald, serving with the Royal Engineers in the Crimean War, was reported in the Inverness Courier as having received an annuity of £20 per annum for his gallantry during the siege of Sebastopol. He was later awarded the Victoria Cross with its then pension of £10 per annum. It is not recorded that Colour Sergeant MacDonald was allowed to receive both annuities.

In conclusion, the award of the Victoria Cross always came with instant recognition for all recipients, however in a very short period the exploits of these men disappeared into the mists of the human mind.

CHAPTER 1

THE MEDAL

When the London Gazette of the 11 October 1982 announced the awards of the Victoria Cross to 2 members of the Parachute Regiment for particular acts of gallantry during the operations to recapture the Falkland Islands from Argentinian forces, it came as no real surprise certainly as far as the award to Colonel "H" Jones was concerned. The award to Sergeant Ian MacKay of the same regiment was totally out of the blue as far as the general public was concerned because the Falklands War was at the time the most accessible for the British public in terms of them being aware of what was happening at the war front on a daily basis. To many of the public the real heroes of this conflict were those media men who during the conflict became household names. With these reports coming back to Britain of events as they were actually happening the public were made aware of some particular acts of gallantry which resulted in talk in several newspapers of Victoria Crosses being won, how this contrasts with the situation 126 years previously.

On the London Gazette of Tuesday 24 February 1857 the following preceded the citations of 85 of the 111 men who had been awarded the Victoria Cross for acts of gallantry during the operations against the Russians in the Crimea:'

"The Queen has been graciously pleased to signify her intention to confer the decoration of the Victoria Cross on the undermentioned officers and men of Her Majesty's Navy and Marines and officers, non-commissioned officers and men of Her Majesty's Army who have been recommended to Her Majesty for that decoration in accordance with the rules laid down in Her Majesty's warrant of Twenty Ninth of January 1856."

The situation was not dissimilar to that of 1982 in that a major war had just finished and the public for the very first time had been kept informed by the press as to what was happening far from Britains shores. William Howard Russell's reports from the front in the Crimea to the readers of "The Times" for all their novelty had enthralled all who had even the slightest interest in these events so far away.

The decoration was not founded until after the war in the Crimea had ended. It had been a war which had started as "popular beyond belief" and ended with disillusionment fuelled by the regular reports about the discomfort and deprivation being experienced by the troops. By that time most, if not all, of the population had turned against the conduct of the campaign.

The British Army and Navy had for many decades fought in all corners of the world against any tribe or indeed nation who dared to stand up against the might of Britain or her colonial interests. During these campaigns British soldiers and sailors performed many acts of bravery. At this time unless the act was performed by an Officer it usually lead to little or no recognition. There was in the system means whereby Officers and gentlemen who had the courage and performed outstandingly were often rewarded in such a way that their social status was enhanced. The Generals often received Knighthoods or even Dukedoms and the lower ranks of Officer could even have a Brevet rank bestowed upon them. Throughout this time there was no award that could be bestowed upon the ordinary soldier. As is the case in every army the majority of those who actually fight in a battle are the ordinary soldiers consequently the majority of the acts which could be considered as acts of gallantry are likely to be performed by the same ordinary soldiers.

In 1854 after great pressure had been put on the Government of the day the Distinguished Conduct Medal was instituted as a reward to ordinary soldiers and non-commissioned officers for particular acts of gallantry. Welcome as this was in the army there was still agitation that there should be one award for extreme gallantry which could be conferred irrespective of rank or status. Queen Victoria herself took great interest in this concept. Both she and her husband Prince Albert became involved from the very early stages and the final design of the new decoration was only approved after consultation with the Queen and her Consort.

After the royal design had been approved the production of the Cross was passed to Hancocks, the London firm of jewellers. The Queen did not wish her new award to be of monetary value she decided that it should be cast in bronze rather than some precious metal. After Her Majesty had decided upon bronze for the decoration, it seemed appropriate at the time that the metal should come from Russian guns captured during the recent war in the Crimea. On display at Woolwich Barracks in London were several war trophies in the form of cannons and rather than destroying them to get the bronze it was decided to remove only the cascabels from the breeches of the guns (these guns can still be seen at Woolwich Barracks minus these parts robbed to provide bronze for the Victoria Cross).

At first the medals were stamped out in the normal fashion for the time but the Crimean bronze proved to be so hard that the dies continually cracked when placed under pressure. In order to overcome this particular problem it was then decided to melt the bronze down and then pour it into a specially prepared mould. This proved to be a success although the finishing touches were required to be done by hand. This is the method that is still used to this day.

When the first Crosses were made each was in the shape of a Maltese Cross with the centre in the form or a royal crown topped by a lion and having the simple inscription "**FOR VALOUR**" below. Each medal was suspended under a red ribbon for members of the army and a blue ribbon for naval personnel.

The rules for the award were contained in the Royal Warrant published on the 29 January 1856 and they made it clear that in order to gain the decoration the recipient must be outstandingly brave and have performed an act or acts of the most conspicuous gallantry in the face of an enemy. This has been amended in subsequent warrants to include acts which were performed in the face of great adversity, i.e. the awards to a Surgeon and 4 Private soldiers of the 2nd Battalion of the 24th Regiment of Foot for saving lives at sea during a storm off the Andaman Islands in the Bay of Bengal in May 1867.

After the publication of the Royal Warrant in January 1856 many hundreds of recommendations from both the Army and Navy were received and considered. From all of these recommendations the number was eventually reduced to those first 85 awards announced on Tuesday 24 February 1856. Some of those who were to receive the first Victoria Crosses were no longer alive, having been killed in some subsequent action or died of disease during the war in the Crimea. However on the 26 June 1857 in Hyde Park in London the first investiture for the Victoria Cross took place with sixty two officers and men from both the Army and Navy present before Her Majesty Queen Victoria. In accordance with her wishes when the medal was instituted, she presented them in no particular order of rank, although the Royal Navy had the honour of receiving the first Cross as it is referred to as the Senior Service. The first man to be presented with Her Majesty's decoration was Commander Henry James Raby of the Royal Navy, who whilst serving with the Naval Brigade before Sebastopol on the 18 June 1855 went forward under a very heavy musket fire accompanied by two seamen to rescue a soldier of the 57th Regiment who was lying in an exposed position in front of the Russian guns. This was fitting as the first act to result in the award of the Victoria Cross was performed by Midshipman Charles Davis Lucas also of the Royal Navy. Midshipman Lucas was serving on board HMS Hecla in the Baltic Sea on the 21 June 1854 when during the attack on the Russian forts at Bomarsund in the Aland Islands a shell landed on the deck of the ship and did not explode immediately. Charles Lucas saw the shell land and at once sprang forward and picked up the shell and threw it overboard. Before the device had reached the sea it exploded showering the amazed crew with nothing more than water. As a result of his prompt action all that happened to the sailors was a soaking. When the Captain of the ship saw this action he immediately promoted the young twenty year old sailor to the rank of Lieutenant. The first Scot to receive the medal was Glasgow born soldier John Simpson Knox who had won his Victoria Cross while serving as a Sergeant in the 2nd Battalion of the Scots Fusilier Guards during the Battle of the Alma on the 20 September 1854.

The Queen's interest in her medal remained with her throughout the rest of her life and even in the very last year of her life she was presenting Victoria Crosses to her brave soldiers and sailors.

At the very time when Queen Victoria was presenting the first medals in Hyde Park her soldiers were again involved in another conflict, this time in far off India. In fact as she was presenting these very first medals two more Scots had already performed acts of gallantry which were to result in them being awarded the Victoria Cross.

As the mutiny in India continued it became necessary to amend the rules to include civilian volunteers as being able to receive the decoration. The Royal Warrant of 13 December 1858 allowed non military personnel who as volunteers had borne arms against mutineers, both at Lucknow and elsewhere to be considered eligible to receive the decoration of the Victoria Cross. The first civilian to receive the award was Irishman Thomas Henry Kavanagh of the Bengal Civil Service who during the siege at Lucknow on the 9 November 1857 volunteered to go back into the rebel held part of the town dressed as a native to the camp of Sir Colin Campbell's relieving forces in order that he could lead them back through the town to the beleaguered garrison at the Residency. As before, the first action which resulted in the award of the Victoria Cross to a civilian had taken place before Mr. Kavanagh's bravery and it had taken place during the retreat by British troops from the town of Arrah on the 30 July 1857. Here the Magistrate of Sarun, William Fraser McDonell, a Bengal Civil Servant won his Victoria Cross. Although not a Scot by birth he was the uncle of the twentieth chief of the Clan McDonell of Glengarry in Scotland. His award came as the result of his coolness and great bravery on that date when he climbed out of a boat, in which he and over thirty soldiers were hoping to escape, under an incessant fire from the rebels. With great difficulty he severed the lashings which secured the boat and thus allowed the flow of the river to take the boat and its valuable cargo away from the rebels who were rapidly closing in on them.

The next major change in the rules for awarding the Victoria Cross came after the death of Queen Victoria, when her son King Edward VII amended the rules to allow for acts which resulted in the death of the person performing that act. Up to that time in order to win a Victoria Cross the recipient had to survive. During the war in South Africa against the Boers five posthumous Victoria Crosses were awarded. These appeared in the London Gazette of the 8th of August 1902. Amongst these was the award to Lieutenant Robert James Thomas Digby-Jones of the Royal Engineers. Edinburgh born Lieutenant Jones along with Trooper Albrecht of the Imperial Light Horse had led a small force which had re-occupied the summit of Waggon Hill, near Ladysmith, at a critical moment. Just as the three leading Boers reached the summit he immediately shot dead one of them and the trooper shot the other two. Lieutenant Jones was killed shortly afterwards while engaged with the enemy as he helped to defend the position.

After the war in South Africa had ended the King continued with his mothers interest in her decoration and in the London Gazette of Tuesday the 15 January 1907 it was reported that His Majesty King Edward VII had been graciously pleased to approve the decoration of the Victoria Cross being delivered to the representatives of the officers and men who had been reported in earlier Gazettes as having fallen in the performance of acts of valour and it was notified in these earlier Gazettes that they would have been recommended for the Victoria Cross had they survived. The first of these awards mentioned was that to Dumfries born Private Edward Spence of the 42nd Highlanders whose name had originally appeared in the Gazette of the 27 May 1859, where it was recorded that had he survived Private Spence would certainly have been recommended for the Victoria Cross. He along with Lance Corporal Thompson of the same Regiment volunteered during the attack on Fort Ruhya in India on the 15 April 1858, to assist Captain Cafe, the Commanding Officer of the 4th Punjab Rifles, in bringing in from the top of the glacis (the outer sloping bank of the fortifications) the body of Lieutenant Willoughby. Private Spence dauntlessly placed himself in an exposed position in order to cover the rescue party carrying away the body. He died on the 17 April from the effects of his wounds he received on that occasion. The Scots born soldier thus became the first winner of a posthumous Victoria Cross. In the great conflicts to come during the twentieth century the occasions in which posthumous awards were made increased to the extent that nowadays there is about a fifty-fifty chance of an award being posthumous. This is confirmed by the fact that six of the eleven awards made since the end of World War Two have been made posthumously.

During the early discussions with Queen Victoria she made it very clear that the decoration which was to bear her name should have little or no monetary value. The Royal Warrant of January 1856 allowed for the payment of an annual pension of £10 and an additional £5 if a bar to the decoration was awarded. However the plight of one of Scotland's most famous Victoria Cross heroes, Piper George Findlater of the Gordon Highlanders was one of the reasons why an embarrassed government ceased the £10 annual pension and replaced it in 1959 with a £100 tax free annuity. After he had won his Cross at the storming of the 600 foot hill known as the Dargai Heights, where he continued to inspire the Gordon Highlanders to capture the hill after he himself had been shot through both legs. The Highlanders had captured the hill in only 30 minutes after the might of the army had struggled for over 5 hours. After he had come out of hospital where he had been presented with his Victoria Cross by the Queen herself, Piper Findlater in spite of being somewhat of a national hero was forced to play his bagpipes in the streets in order to earn enough money with which to support his family. Piper Findlater was indeed fortunate in that he had his bagpipes with which he could earn a living – others were not so fortunate.

Among those was Private David MacKay, who originally came from Thurso in Caithness, to enlist in the 93rd Highlanders in December 1850. He served with the regiment during the Crimean War and was one of those who formed that famous "Thin Red Line tipped with steel" before Balaclava in October 1854. It was during his regiments service in India, as part of the army sent to quell the Mutiny, that he was awarded the Victoria Cross for his personal bravery in capturing the colour of a rebel regiment. Although wounded at the capture of the Shah Nujjiff at Lucknow the day after he won his decoration, he continued to serve in India. As a result of that wound received at Lucknow he was forced to leave the army in 1861. After returning to civilian life he moved with his wife and family to Lesmahagow in Lanarkshire, where he died at the age of 50 and was buried in a pauper's grave. Forgotten for almost 100 years until someone concerned about one of Scotland's heroes contacted the Argyll and Sutherland Highlanders about Private MacKay. As a result of this the regiment, the successors to the 93rd Highlanders, presented a plaque for his grave in recognition of the place that this winner of the highest award for gallantry has in the history of this famous regiment.

Private MacKay was one of many soldiers who had to sell his medal in order to live. Queen Victoria when involved in the early design of the medal made it clear that she did not wish her decoration to be made from any precious metal as she did not wish it to detract from the intention of the award in the first place i.e. that it should be awarded on an equal basis irrespective of rank or title. This to some extent went against these winners who because of circumstances which were in the most cases beyond their control had to sell their medal. They could only attain a value commensurate with the scarcity of the medal. Even in fairly recent times when the pension attached to the award was a little more generous recipients often had to sell their decorations in order to survive. The most famous of these was Flight Sergeant John Hannah. Sergeant Hannah from Paisley in Renfrewshire was one of the first members of the Royal Air Force to win the Victoria Cross during the Second World War. In winning his medal he had sustained terrible injuries and burns which were so severe he had to be invalided out of the service. When he was fit Sergeant Hannah would tour the wartime music halls and relate to the public how he had won his Victoria Cross. As a direct result of his injuries his health rapidly began to deteriorate and even before he died in 1947 at the early age of 25 his medal was being considered for sale. Since his death his medal has changed hands more than once, each time the price reflecting that he was the youngest recipient of the Victoria Cross during the Second World War.

Victoria Crosses coming up for sale today can fetch anything from £10,000 upwards, in fact the medal awarded to Private Findlater of Dargai Heights fame became available for sale in May 1991 when it was expected to fetch over £35,000. Piper Findlaters family took action to have the sale stopped and sought legal advice on how to have the medal returned back into the family ownership. As recently as September 1992 the medals, including the Victoria Cross, won by First World War Pilot Major Edward Mannock were sold for a record £132,000 at Sotherby's.

How times have changed, in 1909 two officers serving with the 2nd Battalion of the Hampshire Regiment in South Africa came across the medals, including the Victoria Cross, of Private Thomas

Lane of the 67th Regiment. Private Lane had won his decoration for displaying great gallantry in swimming the ditches which surrounded the North Taku Fort in China on the 21 August 1860. Although his medal had been officially returned after his name had been removed from the Register of the Victoria Cross under Clause 15 of the Royal Warrant dated 29 January 1856 for desertion. This medal which was purchased to redeem a pawn shop pledge for £9 proved to be genuine and remains in the possession of the Hampshire Regiment to this day.

By the 1950's collectors were prepared to pay up to £200 for medals which appeared for sale and by the 1970's medals were fetching well into 4 figures. Today as I have already said medals belonging to Victoria Cross winners fetch vast amounts which bear no resemblance to the cost of producing the medal. Also in 1992 a medal belonging to a young pilot of Bomber Command, who had died in winning his Cross, was sold for £52,000. Fortunately in recent times collectors who bid for and are successful in obtaining the Victoria Cross of some forgotten hero have in many cases presented their acquisition to the parent museum of the recipients regiment or service. This certainly the case for the other Victoria Cross which attributed to Private Lane of the 67th Regiment. The medal came up for sale in Glasgow in 1984 and after being purchased for £3,800 was presented to the Regimental Museum of the Royal Hampshire Regiment to be displayed alongside the other medals acquired by the museum almost 80 years previously. This display of 2 Victoria Crosses both confirmed as genuine and belonging to the same man is unique in the annals of the Victoria Cross

Also the medals belonging to Able Seaman Edward Robinson of the Royal Navy who won his Victoria Cross at Lucknow in India on 13 March 1858, for extinguishing a fire in some sandbags on top of defensive earthworks when the mutineers were within 50 yards of him, came up for sale in London in the early 1970's and at that time fetched £3,500. The purchaser at the time said he would make the Victoria Cross available to the National Maritime Museum at Greenwich.

The attraction to collectors of Victoria Crosses is that of scarcity and as long as the circumstances in which the decoration can be won remain as stringent it seems unlikely that in this time of world peace that there will be opportunities for members of Her Majesties Armed Forces to win this most coveted of all decorations. It is almost 50 years since the last Scot won a Victoria Cross and over 10 years since the last awards were won in the Falklands. In this time not a year has gone by in which some British soldier has died on active service and as the circumstances in which a Victoria Cross can be awarded remain at such an exceptionally high standard reflecting the greatest gallantry, it is increasingly unlikely that new names will ever be added to the Roll of Honour of the Victoria Cross in the numbers which were added between 1914 and 1919.

CHAPTER 2

VICTORIA'S HEROES REMEMBERED

THE CRIMEA 1854/55

It was on the 28th of February 1854 that Her Majesty Queen Victoria signed the document which caused Great Britain and her Allies to be at war with the Russian Empire. Thus Britain was committed to the first European war in which her troops had been involved since the defeat of the French under Napoleon Bonaparte and as history was to deem it would be her only European campaign until the British Expeditionary Force landed in Europe in August 1914.

The roots of the war in the Crimea went back to 1852 when Emperor Napoleon III was enthroned in Paris. During that year French diplomatic pressure had been put on the Turkish Government to recognise the historical claims of the Latin Church in the Holy Land (which at that time was part of the vast Ottoman Empire) to help with the running of the holy places. As a result of this pressure, by the end of 1852 the Latin Church was in full control of shrines such as the Church of the Nativity in Bethlehem. In January 1853 the Tsar Nicholas I of Russia decided that political pressure and threats of force as had been exhibited by France on behalf of the Latin Church would be needed to establish the same sort of rights for the Greek Church.

In order to exert such pressure Russian troops were moved up to the borders of the Russian controlled principalities of Moldavia and Wallachia. An act made all the more threatening because the Russians had withdrawn only two years previously to defuse a dangerous confrontation. The Tsar feeling that this show of strength gave him the upper hand then sent his special envoy Prince Menshikov to Constantinople to negotiate a treaty which would allow Russia to protect the interests of the Greek Orthodox Church, a similar privilege to that already enjoyed by France on behalf of the Latin Church.

The Tsar's hopes of a treaty without bloodshed were dashed when in both London and Paris there were violent demonstrations against Russia's ambitions in Europe, as the Ottoman Empire had boundaries with Europe. The dispute was dragging on and Prince Menshikov demanded a final answer from the Sultan, while both sides continued with their warlike preparations. The question being asked was "Will the Tsar precipitate hostilities in the face of growing opposition?" Both Great Britain and France had pledged their support to the Sultan of Turkey. At this time the British fleet had sailed for the Mediterranean in a gesture of support for Turkey. In July of 1853 the Russian troops finally crossed the borders into the principalities of Moldavia and Wallachia as efforts were still being made to secure peace. After these efforts by Austria as a mediator ended in failure Turkey declared war on Russian October 1853. By November the British and French fleets had passed through the Dardanelles into the Black Sea as a show of Strength. In December the Russians finally declared war on Turkey and in a single act of aggression had attacked and destroyed a Turkish Naval squadron at Sinope on the southern shores of the Black Sea.

Public opinion at home and in Europe was so intense that the French Emperor Napoleon III felt he had to react to this threat by not allowing anyone to tread on his toes and as a result of that document signed by Queen Victoria on that last day of February 1854 both Britain and France as allies of Turkey were committed to a war with Russia. Shortly afterwards Russia, under a threat from Austria, because of Russian troops on the River Danube, withdrew her troops from the principalities of Moldavia and Wallachia. However this chance of major peace was not grasped as both sides did not wish to lose face. European public opinion was still very much against Russia and felt that she had to be put in her place in order to extinguish her ambitions in Eastern Europe.

The trumpets of war were sounding loud and clear throughout Europe and the patriotic spirit which was gripping everyone had even reached the Queen of Britain. In a reply to the King of Prussia who had tried once more to reach a peaceful solution she said "Beware of entrance to a quarrel; but being in bear it that the opposer may beware of thee" Later she was to describe the war as "Popular beyond belief"

William Howard Russell, who was to become the father of modern war correspondence, on being told by his editor in the Times that he was to be sent to the front expected to be home by Easter. Mr Russell had left London on the 22nd of February and had travelled to Malta with the Brigade of Guards. The troops had been sent to the island to remind the Tsar that Britain was prepared to commit her soldiers to battle if necessary. The British troops landed at Valetta on the 2nd of March 1854.

Meanwhile the Allies and their fleets had control of the waters of the Black Sea and continued to show off their strength at various points along the Russian coastline. In June 1854 in the Baltic Sea the British Fleet had destroyed the Russian held forts at Bomarsund in the Aland Islands. It was during this action that a young Midshipman named Charles Lucas serving on board HMS Hecla had thrown overboard a live shell with fuse still burning from the deck of his ship. This was done with complete disregard for his own safety. The shell exploded as it hit the water causing no more damage to the ship than a soaking for some of the crew. Charles Lucas was immediately promoted to the rank of Lieutenant. This proved to be the earliest action for which a Victoria Cross was awarded. With the final destruction of the Russian Baltic fleet at Gustarfson the British fleet secured command of that sea and a safe anchorage.

Initially the Allied forces had arrived in small numbers and even at that time a young highland soldier writing home to his local paper in Inverness had told of the great want of comfort for the ordinary soldier when up to sixteen men had to share a single tent and even officers were having to use tents bereft of furniture. As the months rolled by the troops arrived in greater numbers and were encamped in places such as Varna, Gallipoli and throughout the Balkans.

On 7 September 1854 the order came to start the invasion and the fleet left Varna with 10,000 well trained troops on board. After several days sailing they arrived off the Russian coast at Eupatoria in the Crimea. A note was sent to the Mayor of the town urging him to surrender his town. When word was returned the troops landed totally unopposed. After they had grouped in the town the army moved southwards to meet the Russian army which was reported to be in defensive positions at the River Alma, before it was reached the Allies met part of the Russian army at the river before called the Bulganak on 19 September and quickly had them retreating towards their main force. On the following day the order to march was given at 6 o'clock in the morning, and organised as the Allied army was they did not advance until after midday. For many soldiers in both armies it was to be the first time that they would be fired upon in earnest. As the assault on the Russian positions continued in the heat of the afternoon the Guards Division, commanded by the Duke of Cambridge, having crossed the river in almost ceremonial order began to climb the far bank which lead to the heavily defended Great Redoubt. On the final assault on this fortification, the Guards who continued to march towards it in parade ground order attacked the hill known as Kourgane and its Russian defenders. The Scots Fusilier Guards ascended the hill which was already strewn with the bodies, both dead and wounded of the first troops who had attacked the enemy positions. This ghastly sight caused a temporary disarray in the ranks of the Fusilier Guards. The Russian soldiers pursuing the remnants of General Codrington's first Guards Brigade broke into the middle of the Scots Fusilier Guards and tried to seize their Colours, which were carried during the battle by Balcarres born Ensign (later Captain) Robert James Lindsay (fig.32). Ensign Lindsay was awarded the Victoria Cross for his gallant action in standing firm with the Colours when many around him had faltered and who by his example of cool courage had helped very quickly to restore order to the ranks. The same award was also conferred on three more Scots soldiers who had helped reform the ranks after this momentary lapse in discipline. They were Sergeant John Simpson Knox who was born in Glasgow, Sergeant James McKechnie who was born in Paisley and Private William Reynolds from Edinburgh. The announcement of the awards to these men were amongst the first 85 which appeared in the London Gazette of the 24th of February 1857.

Having forced a way forward at incredible speed towards the main Russian port in the Crimea at Sebastopol the Allies were unable to capitalise on their success and fight their way to the very gates of that town. Instead they embarked on what was to be a long and circuitous route around Sebastopol to establish a base in the town of Balaclava where the British and French fleets had already gained a foothold. This important delay was made full use of by the Russian garrison in Sebastopol and allowed them time to prepare for a siege which was to last to the very end of the war. The detour around

Sebastopol had come about because the Allied spies had reported that the next two rivers to be crossed on the road to Sebastopol would be defended by the enemy in even greater numbers. So on hearing this it was decided upon the flanking movement which was to lengthen the war immeasurably and at the time avoid high numbers of casualties.

As the Russians settled down for a long siege the Allies began to prepare to force the town to surrender through starvation and bring about the reason for the invasion in the first place, the destruction of Sebastopol. With Naval supremacy already established and the armies starting to tighten the screw there was no real reason to expect the siege to last very long. Those vital days and hours lost within sight of the northern wall of Sebastopol were to prove costly as the campaign ran its course.

Reconnaissance on 13 October indicated that Russian troops were massing in the vicinity of the town of Balaclava so Sir Colin Campbell and his Highland Brigade was sent to the area. Sir Colin immediately set about improving the defences around Balaclava by establishing a series of earthworks, redoubts and trenches.

On the morning of 25 October a large column of Russian troops appeared without warning in front of the Turkish soldiers dug in beside the Sebastopol to Kamara road. Hopelessly outnumbered and outgunned the Turks retreated in the face of such overwhelming odds. The Heavy Brigade under the command of General Sir James Scarlett, a man in his mid fifties and experiencing battle for the first time was sent to the rescue of the Turks, who by the time of their arrival, had already departed the field of conflict. After quickly assessing the situation General Scarlett gave the order for his heavy cavalry to charge the advancing Russian column. When the enemy were engaged it became apparent after only a few minutes that the Russians were showing signs of wavering and in less than 10 minutes were in full retreat. It was during this charge by the Heavy Brigade that the next two Scottish winners of the Victoria Cross won their awards. The first was won by Musselburgh born Sergeant Major John Grieve of the 2nd Dragoons who during the heat of the battle had galloped to the rescue of an officer who had been dismounted and was fighting off some Russian cavalrymen who had surrounded him. When he rushed to the officers rescue Sergeant Major Grieve drove off the attackers after he had severed the head of one of them. The other award of that day went to Edinburgh man Sergeant Henry Ramage, also of the 2nd Dragoons, for several acts of gallantry on the day of the battle of Balaclava, including the rescue of Private MacPherson of his own regiment who had been surrounded by seven of the enemy, and for bravery later on in the day when the men of the Heavy Brigade were involved in covering the retreat of those survivors of the ill fated charge of the Light Brigade. Although best remembered for the charge of the Light Brigade, the Battle of Balaclava had all but been won as a result of the actions of General Scarlett's Heavy Brigade and Sir Colin Campbell's Highlanders.

After the end of the battle it was soon apparent that the Crimean winter was beginning to lay its siege on the Allied armies. The armies which had left for the Crimea in the height of a west European summer was not in the least prepared for the rigours of an eastern European winter. Soon the weather was beginning to take a toll of fighting men far in excess of that taken by the Russian cannons.

Before that first winter took its final grip, on 5 November, a Russian force, trying to break the siege at Sebastopol came from the direction of Balaclava in an attempt to force a way through the army surrounding the town. For days the Allied commanders had been aware of what had seemed like enemy troop concentrations behind the besiegers dug in around the outside of Sebastopol. In the early morning mist there was nothing to indicate that the enemy was about to make an attack. About six o'clock in the morning there was the sound of sporadic rifle fire, which in itself was not too unusual, but by seven o'clock it was reported that the British defenders on the Inkerman Ridge were engaged with a large Russian force of more than 15,000 men. The British force was only 4,000 strong and bitter hand to hand fighting ensued before reinforcements could arrive. In the confusion of the close quarter battle fought in dense fog Private Thomas Beach, from Dundee, and serving in the 55th Regiment, rescued Lieutenant Colonel Carpenter of the 41st Regiment who was lying wounded on the ground and was surrounded by several Russians. He stayed with and protected this officer until men from the 41st Regiment arrived to carry him to safety. For his devotion to the officer Private Beach became the next Scots born winner of the Victoria Cross. Another Scot was similarly decorated for gallantry at the

Battle of Inkerman on that day. He was Private John McDermond, who was born in Clackmannanshire who also won his cross for the rescue of an officer who had been wounded and was being attacked by Russian soldiers. Private McDermond was a soldier in the 47th Regiment.

With the onset of the winter both sides settled down to the daily routine of making the laying of a siege as comfortable as possible. The work of harassment went on by both day and night and it was during one of these raids into the enemy's rifle pits that Lieutenant William James Cuninghame, who was later to become a Member of Parliament for the town of his birth, Ayr, was serving with the 1st Battalion of the Rifle Brigade won another of Scotland's Victoria Crosses. On the night of 20 November 1854 Lieutenant Cuninghame and Lieutenant Bourchier of the same regiment advanced on the enemy's rifle pits with the intention of driving them from the position. In the bitter hand to hand fighting for possession of the pits the officer leading the raid was killed and the two lieutenants continued to press home the attack and held the hard won position all through the night and into the next day when they were relieved. For their leadership throughout the night and day both men were decorated with the Victoria Cross.

Meanwhile the troops in the trenches had spent a most uncomfortable winter trying to maintain the pressure on the enemy garrison within the walls and earthworks of the besieged town of Sebastopol. William Howard Russell continued to send back reports from the front to his readers in Britain. The war which had started by being "popular beyond belief" was beginning to turn sour and the people back home were starting to agitate for better conditions for the men at the front. This was at a time when Highland soldiers writing home from the Crimea sometimes found it necessary to write on pieces of cloth because note paper was not available. Back in Britain public meetings were being held in all parts of the country to promote the establishment of a Patriotic Fund to help make life a little more comfortable for the troops. The situation was not helped by the disastrous events of 14 November when thirty five ships were lost in a great storm with the loss of clothing for 40,000 men and also the loss of 144 lives when a troopship was also sunk. The great storm did not cause the winters discontent but it certainly led to a winter of great discomfort for many throughout all of the ranks. It also caused politicians at home to begin to criticise the conduct of the war and in January 1855 a motion was put before Parliament demanding that a Committee of Enquiry be set up to look into the conditions of the army in the Crimea.

Meanwhile the siege of Sebastopol continued throughout the rest of the winter and as spring arrived so increased the intensity of the operations against the Russians. The death of Tsar Nicholas I made no difference to the enemy's attitude and the war of attrition continued unabated. The spring offensive coupled with the continuing artillery bombardment meant that the defensive positions were constantly in need of repair. During April 1855 this work resulted on a further two Victoria Crosses being awarded to Scots born soldiers. On 13 April, the first of these was won by another Paisley born soldier, Private Samuel Evans of the 19th Regiment for his work in repairing damaged embrasures under a severe fire from the enemy riflemen. Also on 19 April during this period of intense activity Inverness born Royal Engineer Colour Sergeant Henry MacDonald became the second Scot that month to receive the Victoria Cross for his courage and determination after having been left as the most senior rank in charge, when all the officers had been disabled by wounds. He continued to lead the teams involved in repairing saps in spite of the attention being received during the repeated attacks by the enemy.

The time went by most slowly and even a conference in Vienna, held in the same month, aimed at ending the war ended in rejection by Russia of the demands of the Allies. The Russian delegates left the conference saying "Russia would rather risk the consequences of war than yield her dominance in the Black Sea"

Back at the war front the bombardment of Sebastopol continued and sorties into the enemy's trenches also continued. It was on the night of 11 May that Captain Thomas de Courcy Hamilton, who had been born in Stranraer in July 1825, led a band of men of his Regiment, the 68th, and boldly charged a vastly superior force of Russian riflemen and drove them from the battery they were defending. For this action Captain Hamilton was awarded the Victoria Cross and subsequently was awarded the Legion d'Honneur by the French government.

Later in May, Her Majesty Queen Victoria, presented Crimean War Medals to mainly disabled and wounded war veterans who had been sent home as a result of those wounds received in the many battles and skirmishes of the war thus far.

As the second summer of the war arrived the attitude which had prevailed during the winter disappeared and was replaced by one which has been described as "reminiscent of a country fair."

On 18 June after what was one of the heaviest bombardments of the war the attack on the fort known as the Redan began after a party of Highlanders from the 93rd Regiment, led by their Adjutant Lieutenant William McBean had gone up to the fort and had not been challenged. Taking this as a sign that the Redan was not occupied the attack was led by storming parties including men of the Highland Brigade. William Russell of the Times reported that the assault was to be made with five columns. In the confusion only three actually advanced when they were meant to and were driven back with terrible losses. Very few even reached the defensive ditch which surrounded the fort. The disaster of this attack on the Redan resulted in the award of thirteen Victoria Crosses of which three were won by Scots born soldiers. The first of these went to Edinburgh born Lieutenant William Hope of the 7th Regiment, who after the troops of the storming parties had retreated in the morning of the 18 June was informed by a senior Non-Commissioned Officer that the Adjutant of the Regiment, Lieutenant Hobson, was lying wounded outside the trenches in sight of the Russian guns. Lieutenant Hope went out and found where the officer was lying partially hidden by an agricultural drainage ditch which ran towards the left flank of the Redan. When he tried to move him it was impossible without the aid of a stretcher so he once more ran back in face of the enemy guns. Having procured a stretcher he again ran across the open ground swept by gunfire and this time was able to bring the Adjutant to safety.

The next award was won by Colour Sergeant Peter Leitch, from Kinross for conspicuous gallantry in the storming of the fort when he and his Engineers formed a bridge across a ditch in order that the ladder parties could proceed to the walls. The bridge was formed by tearing down material from the gabions in the parapet and filling up the ditch. He continued to do this until he was wounded and was forced to retire. The last Scottish Victoria Cross winner of the day like Colour Sergeant Leitch was also a member of the Royal Engineers. He was Sapper John Perie, who was born in Huntly in Aberdeenshire. Sapper Perie's award was for invaluable service throughout the day of the attack, in particular when he led a party of sailors who were in a ladder party at the beginning of the storming. Later in the day he rescued a wounded man who was lying exposed to the Russian Sharpshooters. This particular act was carried out in spite of having received a bullet wound in his side.

After the failure of the attack in June there were no more major assaults by the British, but the siege still continued with the same intensity. Roderick McGregor a crofter from Inverness was awarded his medal for courageous conduct throughout the whole of the month of July when he was employed as a sharpshooter in the advanced trenches. He is particularly mentioned for his behaviour in dislodging two Russian sharpshooters who were causing some casualties in the British lines. Private McGregor was serving with the 2nd Battalion of the Rifle Brigade.

The last three Scottish winners of the Crimean war were Corporal John Ross, who was born in Stranraer, Colour Sergeant James Craig who was born in Perth and Captain Charles Lumley who was born in Forres, Morayshire. Colour Sergeant Craig received his decoration for having volunteered and personally collected other volunteers to go out on the night of 6 September 1855 to look for Captain Buckley of the Scots Fusilier Guards who was reported to be lying wounded in front of the Redan. Sergeant Craig with the assistance of a drummer found the officer who by that time had died and brought his body back to their own lines. In the performance of this act the Colour Sergeant was himself wounded. Corporal Ross serving with the Royal Engineers received his medal for distinguished conduct on 3 occasions between 21 July and 8 September at which time he crawled forward to the Redan during the night and reported it having been abandoned on which information its occupation by British troops took place. The last Scots born winner during the Crimean War was Captain Charles Lumley serving in the 97th Regiment. He distinguished himself by his bravery during the assault on the Redan on 8 September by being one of the first inside the fort where he immediately engaged some Russian gunners who were in the act of reloading a cannon. Two of the enemy were at once shot dead by the Scot and before he could deal with the others he was temporarily stunned by a large stone thrown at him. On his recovery his immediate reaction was to encourage others of his regiment who had followed him into the fort. Whilst he was cheering and waving his sword about he was disabled by a wound in the mouth from a musket ball.

When news came of the fall of Sebastopol after the French had succeeded in capturing that other great fort, the Malakoff, the British captured the Redan and after much desperate fighting the war came to a virtual end. The Council of War in the Crimea decided that further operations against the enemy had to be abandoned for the winter and arrangements were made for comfortable accommodation for the troops. This effectively ended the war and on 1 February 1856 the Russians accepted a preliminary peace as a result of the additional threat from Austria to declare war on Russia. The final settlement on the war took place in Paris during February and March of that year. The final settlement of the Eastern Question, which had been the primary objective of the Allies, resulted. The Allies had secured the objectives over which they had fought, Turkey remained intact and Russia was denied all rights over the Holy places in the Ottoman Empire.

During the period of the conflict a total of 111 Victoria Crosses were awarded and 19 of these went to Scottish born soldiers.

PERSIA 1856/57

In the nineteenth century Persia was best described as an under-developed country which was being exploited by both Great Britain and Russia. As Britain expanded her Indian Empire almost to the very borders of Russia Afghanistan became the corridor which kept these two great nations apart. Although Russia had been defeated by the Allies, including Great Britain in the Crimea it did not prevent her scheming in the East. In the autumn of 1856 the Shah of Persia had attacked the Afghan city of Herat. When the city was eventually captured Britain believing that the Russians were behind the Shah's aggression sent a force to establish a foothold on Persian soil.

In December 1856 a small British force attacked and captured the Persian port of Bushire. The idea behind the attack was to establish a base from which reinforcements could be landed to march inland and put to an end the threat from Persia. Persia remained a threat as long as her troops occupied the neutral state of Afghanistan which bordered the Indian Empire. It was during the fighting for the port of Bushire on 9 December 1856, that Fort William born John Augustus Wood serving with the 20th Bombay Native Infantry won his Victoria Cross. Captain Wood led a company of Grenadiers on the assault of the fort which protected the port of Bushire. He was in fact the first man onto the parapet of the fort where he was immediately attacked by a large number of the Persian garrison. A volley of muskets was fired at a very close range and this officer was hit no less than seven times. Without hesitation he threw himself onto the group who had fired upon him and set about attacking them. By the time the remainder of his men had caught up with him he had killed the enemy leader. At this point the rest of his Grenadiers arrived and quickly overcame all opposition.

As soon as the base at Bushire had been set up the main British force disembarked at the port without the loss of a single man as the result of enemy action. The British force consisted of two Infantry Divisions and a Cavalry Brigade under the command of Lieutenant General Sir James Outram. On 3 February this force moved inland in a search for the enemy. They soon realised that the Persians were massing troops in order to try and recapture Bushire. Having seized the advantage by moving out to meet the enemy the column advanced across the desert for two days and nights without coming into contact with them. During this march the troops who had for the most part come from the plains of India had to endure the ravages of dust storms and thunderstorms, which were to be expected in Persia in the middle of the winter. On the third day the enemy were sighted and they immediately ran into the hills when they saw how well the British soldiers were equipped. The next day it was decided not to follow the enemy into the hills as they would then have the advantage over the British. On the evening of 7 February orders were received to march back to Bushire. They set out and had only gone about 15 miles when word came that the rearguard had been attacked by the enemy near the village of Khoosab. The 78th Highlanders as part of the First Infantry Division were ordered to return to give support to the beleaguered rearguard. The enemy had surrounded the British and were showering them with not very effective although accurate artillery fire. The column was subjected to an almost continual barrage throughout the night. During this bombardment the British lost only a handful of men and the men of the 78th did not lose a single man.

In the light of day the situation was quickly assessed by the Highlanders, and the Native Infantry, who had taken part in the original capture of Bushire in the previous December, advanced against the enemy at double march speed. The infantry advance was as steady as could be expected on any exercise in spite of being showered by grapeshot and musket fire.

The Persian troops who had been trained by two former Scottish officers proved to be worthy adversaries in the early part of the battle. When the Cavalry attacked the Persians they immediately formed themselves into their version of the British square in order to withstand the mounted attack. These squares were eventually broken down and it was during one of these being destroyed that a second Scot was to win his Victoria Cross. At the height of the fighting at Khoosab Lieutenant John Grant Malcolmson (fig.1), who had been born in Inverness on 9 February 1835 followed his Adjutant of the 3rd Bombay Light Cavalry. Lieutenant Arthur Moore into a square of approximately 500 Persians. The Adjutant's horse had been killed at the very moment that he had leapt over the heads of the enemy into the square. The dismounted Adjutant was trying to fight his way out of the square with a broken sword when Lieutenant Malcolmson saw his plight and fought his way towards his dismounted colleague. He was able to get him onto the horse beside himself and they galloped away to safety. The British and Native Infantry following close behind were able to fix bayonets to disperse the enemy in all directions, who left behind over thirty artillery pieces and 700 dead. The total British casualties for the engagement was 77 killed and wounded.

The victorious force now returned to the coast where they remained until early March when a small force of 4,000 men including the Highlanders left Bushire in ships to attack the regrouped Persian army at Mohomrah about twenty miles up the River Euphrates. On their arrival the enemy were not in the mood for another fight and fled abandoning their position without putting up any resistance. The army remained at Mohomrah until May 1857 when they embarked for India. On their arrival in Bombay they were greeted with the news that the Native army in India had Mutinied.

During the six months of the campaign in Persia a total of three Victoria Crosses were awarded and two of these went to Scottish born soldiers.

INDIA 1857/59

Lord Roberts perhaps the greatest hero of Victorian Britain, winner of a Victoria Cross during the Indian Mutiny, wrote in his book "Forty One Years in India" that the causes of the rebellion in India were sevenfold and these were:-

1. The higher caste Indian soldiers felt their religion, Hinduism was in danger of being dissolved into a form less potent by the infiltration of Christianity.
2. Rumours that the new cartridges to be introduced were covered with a grease which was made from a mixture of the unclean pig and cow fat.(The soldiers had to bite the end of the cartridge before loading the rifle.)
3. The annexation of the Province of Oudh by Lord Dalhousie caused a situation whereby other natives treated the people from Oudh poorly because they considered them to be the mere slaves of the British.
4. The ordinary Sepoy in the Indian army had a position in the hierarchy which led them to believe that they were a cut above the rest of their countrymen.
5. The British troops were very much in the minority in such a large country. They were in fact less than one tenth of the total of native troops.
6. Late in 1856 it became mandatory for Sepoys to serve in other countries. This to the most fervent of the Hindus was another attempt to overturn their beliefs.

7. The attitude of many of the British officers in the Native Army was one of complacency in that they
   were not able to interpret the actions of the men under them as a threat.

Much has been written about the introduction of the new cartridges in early 1857 but the whole
situation was ripe for revolution. Britain had just defeated the greatest threat to world peace and at the
time she was very much regarded as resting on her laurels. Britain also believed that no army least of all
a native army would challenge her domination. There is no doubt that the new Enfield rifle was an
improvement as far as efficiency in action was concerned except for the fact that it entailed the religious
Sepoys putting a cartridge, greased with a mixture of cow and pig fat, into their mouths every time the
rifle was loaded. This was bound to be a recipe for dissatisfaction, as the Hindus believed that the cow
was a sacred beast whereas the pig was considered to be the most unclean. By April 1857 those officers
who were more enlightened and took notice of what their men were doing and saying began to realise
that all was not well. A serious of incidents by individual Sepoys who reacted against the British officers
and tried to enlist the help of their comrades, were in most cases, put down to bouts of madness.

On 8 May 1857 at Meerut over 80 men of the 3rd Bengal Light Cavalry, some of them the heroes of
the Battle of Khooshab in Persia the previous February, had refused to use the new cartridges which
were the subject of so much rumour. These men were court martialled and found guilty of
insubordination and were publicly humiliated in front of the rest of the garrison as an example of what
would happen in similar circumstances.

Two days later on 10 May the majority of the rest of the 3rd Cavalry took the law into their own
hands and freed the prisoners and returned to the fort, accompanied by the men of the 20th Native
Infantry, also veterans of the expedition against the Persians. When they reached the garrison the
Commanding Officer of the 11th Native Infantry, Colonel John Finnis, came out in an attempt to talk
the men back into their barracks. As his body fell to the ground riddled with shot from the muskets of
the Sepoys of the 20th Infantry, the Mutiny began.

Had the army of India been officered by men of the calibre who were to shine through in the months
to come there is no doubt that this very local mutiny would have been suppressed. However this was
not the case and even as the original mutineers made their way to Delhi to crown Bahadur Shah,
Emperor of Hindustan, there was no real attempt to pursue the relatively small band of mutineers as
they made their way to Delhi. In a very short time the garrisons at Meerut and Delhi had joined the
revolution. As the mutineers gathered in numbers so did the slaughter of civilians.

By the end of May 1857 India was in a state of high alert and many more of the native troops had
now joined in the rebellion. Reinforcements were starting to arrive from home and abroad to build
upon the relatively small number of regiments which could be trusted. The 78th Highlanders had
arrived back in India from their recent campaign in Persia and other regiments like the 93rd
Highlanders were diverted to the seat of the rebellion from service in China in order to quell the
mutiny. As British troops had only recently completed the defeat of Russia and were very much seen to
be resting on their past glories, many battalions were not ready to embark for India in May when the
mutiny actually began. Due to this lack of readiness by the vast majority of regiments the momentum
of revolution became almost unstoppable, however by June 1857 the numbers of non native troops had
increased significantly.

After the initial insurrection at Meerut the mutineers quickly moved on through the countryside and
headed for the city of Delhi where they were joined by more native troops, took the city and proclaimed
the King of Delhi the new Emperor of the homeland of Hindustan.

Although the garrison at Delhi had previously been warned of the earlier events at Meerut nothing
was done to prepare for their arrival until the rebels actually arrived swollen in numbers by many
thousands of native troops who had already been disenchanted by the insistence that the new grease
covered cartridges had to be used. They needed little or no encouragement to join the growing band of
mutineers who arrived unopposed at the city as the European inhabitants were making their way to the

many camps of the British regiments. Any civilian, whether or not they had a military connection, who was left in the city was soon to be the target of an orgy of blood similar to that which was the fate of those Europeans at Meerut.

On 12 June at a tower above Delhi, known as the "Flagstaff", a large group of non-military personnel had sought refuge. It was here that Lieutenant Thomas Cadell of the 2nd Bengal Fusiliers won his Victoria Cross when the position was attacked by a large body of rebel soldiers. The defenders, the 75th regiment and the 2nd Bengal Fusiliers, were forced to retire inside the defences of the tower. Cockenzie born Lieutenant Cadell went out under a very severe fire from the enemy's muskets and rescued a bugler of his own regiment, the 2nd Bengal Fusiliers, from amongst the enemy. Later in the same day he rescued a soldier of the 75th regiment who had earlier in the day been severely wounded and was lying in an exposed position from which he was in grave danger of being cut to pieces by the enemy. All this was done at a time when the enemy were laying down a most effective fire and advancing on the precarious lines of defence at the "Flagstaff".

Having gathered momentum at Delhi, the rebels then headed for the town of Lucknow where they met European defenders who were better prepared for them, at least to the extent that fortifications had been erected in anticipation of trouble sometime before to defend the Residency of the Governor, Sir Henry Lawrence. In June 1857 when the native troops finally mutinied the defenders settled down to what would be the major siege of the whole campaign.

On 30 June Lieutenant Robert Aitken performed the first of a series of acts which were to result in the award of the Victoria Cross for him. On 3 different occasions he went out of the defences into the town under the enemy's loopholes into that part of the town known as "The Captain's Bazaar" and on each occasion brought back a number of bullocks which had been left there. Also on 3 July after the enemy had set fire to an area known as "The Bhoosa Stock" it was feared that the fire would spread to a powder magazine which had been abandoned nearby. Lieutenant Aitken with several other officers again left the defences and went to the area where they cut down several tents which because they were still erected could have given the fire a route to the powder dump. Although this was done at night he was forced to work in the presence of a very bright light emanating from the flames in an area which was attracting musket fire from the enemy.

As the siege continued at Lucknow many more native troops from various regiments had mutinied at many barracks along the Ganges valley.

On 10 July at Kolapore when a strong party of rebels had taken up position in a fortified emplacement near the town, Lieutenant William Alexander Kerr, who was born in Melrose, attached to the Southern Maharrata Irregular Horse, led a small party against the position defended by the mutineers. Although he had no artillery pieces with him he led a group of his horsemen dismounted against a gateway and having forced down that gate gained an entrance. After a sharp and bloody close quarter encounter the attack was successful and all the defenders were killed or captured. For his actions on this occasion Lieutenant Kerr was decorated with the country's highest award for gallantry.

In the meantime a force under Major General Sir Henry Havelock had gathered at Allahabad. When the Scottish contingent had been increased by the arrival of the 78th Highlanders, fresh from their success against the Persians at Khooshab, they moved off to relieve the men, women and children in Cawnpore. Havelock's column after several attempts at relieving the garrison eventually succeeded on 17 July. When the victorious troops entered Cawnpore they found before them evidence of what was to prove one of the greatest atrocities committed against the Europeans in the whole campaign in India. The entire garrison on the promise of a safe passage from the leader of the mutineers, Nana Sahib, surrendered only to be massacred and the bodies of the women and children thrown down a well in the town.

As Sir Henry Havelock's column, numbering less than 1,500 men, continued on its way to relieve Lucknow they came into contact with the enemy at the town of Oonao on 29 July. During the attack on the town, Glasgow born, Lieutenant Andrew Bogle of the 78th Highlanders led men of his regiment into a loopholed house which was strongly defended by determined mutineers. In the fighting Lieutenant Bogle was severely wounded but by his actions his regiment was able to continue its advance through the rebel held town. For his bravery in leading his men against such a position, Lieutenant Bogle became the third Scot to win a Victoria Cross in the Indian Mutiny.

Meanwhile back at the besieged town of Lucknow Lieutenant Robert Aitken was again involved in the defence of the Residency. On the night of 20 August after the enemy had set fire to the Baillie Guard Gate in an attempt to gain entry to the defenders assisted by some loyal Sepoys and a water carrier from his own regiment he succeeded in opening the gate despite the heavy musket fire from the enemy. When the gate was opened he was able to remove the burning wood and straw and thus saved the gate from being burned down depriving the enemy of an entrance into the defences.

As the relieving column was nearing Lucknow it became necessary to wait for reinforcements as the column's strength had almost been halved due to the loss of men not only through enemy action but also through Cholera which had spread rapidly through the soldiers. By September 1857 that original column had all but ceased to be a fighting force and it was only with the arrival of another column commanded by Major General Sir James Outram that the numbers became sufficient to once more be an effective force. Havelock had to relinquish command to his old friend and on the 19th of that month the new column numbering 3,500 men set off for what they hoped would be the lifting of the siege on Lucknow.

As the combined column advanced on Lucknow they came into contact with the mutineers on 21 September. Nearing the town the men of the 90th Light Infantry acting as skirmishers ahead of the main column came upon enemy guns which if not silenced could delay the relief of Lucknow. Lieutenant William Rennie (fig.2), from Elgin, who was in front of the skirmishers quickly realised that the guns had to be silenced. He immediately launched an attack on them before the enemy attempted to drag them to another position. As a result of his swift action the guns were captured and Lieutenant Rennie received the Victoria Cross. Later as the column was reaching Lucknow itself, Lieutenant Rennie once again led a charge of men of the 90th regiment against the enemy who were also forced to abandon their guns.

Having arrived at the outskirts of the town the column entered and immediately became involved in a vicious hand to hand battle for supremacy in the narrow streets of the town. Almost every house was defended by mutineers who having the advantage of knowing every inch of the battle ground were not about to give up easily. By late afternoon of 25 September it became apparent to the relieving forces that they were not going to reach the Residency that evening unless a major last effort was made. In spite of a dispute between Havelock and Outram the column moved onto the Residency and after more close quarter fighting in which about 500 casualties were received the Residency was relieved much to the delight of the now very tired defenders.

At the same time inside Lucknow, Robert Aitken on the night when Major General Havelock's column reached the Residency, led a small band of Sepoys of the 13th Native Infantry against two enemy guns which had been positioned opposite the Baillie Guard Gate. The attack was mounted in order to prevent the mutineers from turning them against the advancing column. After he had completed his attack on the guns he then turned his attention on that part of Lucknow known as the Teree Kotee.

Although it had always been the intention of General Havelock to rescue and remove the defenders from the Residency he was not able to do this as the final assault on those surrounding it had robbed him of much of his force, resulting in the loss of his ability to withdraw as a fighting column. The relieving column was now inside the defences of the Residency and instead of easing the situation with the arrival of the relief forces had in fact worsened the plight by increasing the call on the already limited provisions of the defenders.

Throughout the day of the final entry into the Residency, 25 September 1857, one of Scotland's most famous Victorian soldiers won his Victoria Cross. Born in Ardersier, near Inverness, Lieutenant

Herbert Taylor MacPherson of the 78th Regiment was eventually to reach the rank of Major General and die on active service in Burma in his sixtieth year. Lieutenant MacPherson displayed conspicuous gallantry and heroic leadership for his men during the whole period of the operation to enter into the Residency. He was particularly prominent in his Regiment's capture of two brass nine pounder cannons after a bayonet charge.

On the morning of 26 September the irrepressible Lieutenant Aitken for a fourth time led out a small band of Sepoys against some mutineers who had established themselves in a fortified position within the doorway of the Furreed Buksh Palace. This position was attacked by the Lieutenant and his small band. During the attack some of the rebels tried to make their escape through a small wicket gate in to the palace itself. On seeing this Lieutenant Aitken immediately sprang forward and by sheer strength prevented the door from being closed. He held the door open until some assistance arrived and his assaulting Sepoys were able to enter the palace and after some hard fighting eventually captured it.

As the column was making its last advance against the mutineers surrounding the Residency it was necessary and prudent to leave behind the men wounded from earlier attempts to break through to the defenders. Amongst those left behind to tend to these men was Dunbar born Surgeon Anthony Home of the 90th Regiment. Surgeon Home realising that the column had advanced so far towards the Residency that they would not be coming back very soon, decided to try and catch up with the column with the remnants of the escort left behind to defend the wounded. On the 26 September the gallant Surgeon led the men through the narrow streets of Lucknow in order to try and find the column from which they had been separated. As they fought their way through the streets they were quickly reduced to all but a few stragglers. With so few fit men they were forced to fight their way into a loopholed house from which they hoped to be able to defend themselves. After defending this somewhat precarious position for more than 22 hours Surgeon Home was one of only six men able to fire at the enemy. Being the senior rank the conduct of the defence fell to the Surgeon who during the final stages of their ordeal displayed continuous persevering bravery and admirable conduct in which the safety of the wounded men was ensured. He was awarded a most deserved Victoria Cross.

In the beleaguered Residency many were still dying both from the results of enemy action and from the privations of so many people in such a small area. As the siege continued another Scot serving in the 78th Highlanders performed an act of bravery which resulted in him being awarded the Victoria Cross. In addition to his general conduct throughout the day of the entry into the besieged area he was noted as having at great personal risk rescued from under the very noses of the enemy a private soldier from his own Company who had been lying severely wounded in a very exposed position. This Scot was Colour Sergeant Stewart McPherson who was born in Culross near Dunfermline.

In Lucknow itself the supplies of food and ammunition were in a desperate state and as the days went by the numbers of casualties increased. It became more and more difficult to maintain the previous high standard of hygiene and disease began to take an even greater toll.

On 29 September the brave Lieutenant Aitken who had had little or no respite since the siege began many months previously once more led his men out of the Residency to continue his harassment of the mutineers. On this occasion he volunteered to go out and capture a gun which was pouring down a continuous fire on the defenders. With four of his trusted Sepoys he went through the maze of narrow streets and lanes and eventually found the offending gun. Although fired upon continuously from the surrounding houses the Lieutenant held his ground until a stronger party from the defenders came to his assistance. The gun was removed from its carriage and dragged back into the Residency. Lieutenant Aitken continued with his acts of gallantry until the Residency was again relieved and he was amongst the gallant defenders who were led to safety by the man who was to become the epitome of Scottish Victorian soldiers, Sir Colin Campbell, Lord Clyde. Although his acts of bravery covered the whole period of the siege of Lucknow Lieutenant Aitken's Victoria Cross was one of the last two awards to be gazetted on the 16 April 1863.

While the Mutiny appeared to be centred around the town of Lucknow it was in fact continuing with the same intensity all along the Ganges Valley. On the 28 September at Bolundshadur near Delhi

Lieutenant Robert Blair of the 2nd Dragoon Guards, whilst attached to the 9th Lancers was ordered to take 12 men and a Sergeant and bring in a deserted ammunition waggon. As his party approached the waggon a body of about sixty enemy horsemen came out from a nearby village and attacked Lieutenant Blair and his men. In spite of the suddenness of the attack the Lieutenant without a moments hesitation formed up his men and regardless of the odds charged through the advancing mutineers. Thus making good his escape without the loss of a single man and leaving behind nine of the enemy dead of whom Lieutenant Blair had killed four before he himself was severely wounded in the shoulder. For his actions on this occasion the Linlithgow born soldier was decorated with a well deserved Victoria Cross.

At Futtehpore, near Agra, which lies between Cawnpore and Delhi on the 28 October a Glasgow man serving with the Bengal Artillery became the next Scottish winner of the Victoria Cross when he went to the rescue of a wounded officer of the 38th Regiment of Bengal Native Infantry who was lying in a position exposed to the fire of the enemy. In performing the act Conductor James Miller was so severely wounded that he had to be sent back to hospital at Agra. At the time of the attack at Futtehpore Conductor Miller was attached to a troop of heavy howitzers.

The ordeal for the defenders of Lucknow was set to continue for several more weeks before it was finally relieved by a column mounted by the Commander in Chief in India himself Sir Colin Campbell. On 14 November 1857 this larger column reached the outskirts of Lucknow where the men in light marching order and every man carrying 40 rounds of ammunition were eager for more action. Sir Colin's plan was to take the more circuitous route around the southern edge of the town in order to avoid the waste of men and resources which General Havelock had experienced in the close quarter fighting through the narrow streets and lanes of the town itself. By this flanking march from the Cawnpore road his plan was to capture the palace known as the Dilkoosha and then onto the Martiniere College, which had been founded by Doctor Martin as a school for the children of the Europeans of Lucknow. He believed as these two buildings were the largest in the southern side they were the most likely to be heavily defended. At 9am the column marched forward and met with no opposition until they came within sight of the Dilkoosha, where they saw that the enemy had erected makeshift defences. The mutineers had been taken by surprise at the approach from the south and were in no way prepared for the attack.

As the column approached the palace the volume of fire increased and fierce fighting between the mutineers and men of the 93rd Highlanders ensued. In a very short time the better disciplined Highlanders of Sir Colin's column soon had the enemy retreating from both the Dilkoosha and the Martiniere College across the canal which flowed around the town and over to the far bank of the River Gumti.

The following day the column was again subjected to intense fire from the rebels. After having secured the ground across the canal the column was ready for the assault on the next large building standing in the way of the advance of Sir Colin's troops, the Secundra Bagh. As the leading troops, the 93rd Highlanders emerged from cover of a village nearby where they were met by an intense but ineffective barrage from the rebel gunners. The Highlanders had to take cover less than 100 yards from the very walls of the heavily fortified enemy position. The Scots were pinned down until support from the Bengal Artillery arrived in the form of two heavy 18 pounder cannons which had been dragged into a firing position by a company of the 93rd Highlanders.

Whilst the walls were being bombarded by the Bengal gunners the Highlanders attacked an enemy position in a large serai, which is a place for travellers to stay, opposite the western side of the Secundra Bagh. When this enemy stronghold had been secured it allowed a breach to be forced which Sir Colin Campbell himself considered large enough for a major assault on the fort. The honour of leading the final attack on the Secundra Bagh was given to the men of the 93rd and 78th Highlanders. Although the original breach was only large enough for one man to enter at a time it was secured by a few of the Highlanders entering one at a time and holding back the enemy until support could come through the gap. Then suddenly the main gate of the Bagh burst open and in poured the men of the 78th and 93rd Highlanders with the Commander in Chief, Sir Colin Campbell riding at their head. Once inside the courtyard there was a battle of such ferocity that every room, hallway and staircase was fought over with no quarter being given or asked for. It was reported that not one single mutineer who had been defending the Secundra Bagh was left alive and that the garrison was over 3,000 men strong.

Countless heroic deeds were performed throughout that day and men of the gallant 93rd received six Victoria Crosses in recognition of that Regiments part in the attack on the Secundra Bagh. The first of these was awarded to Thurso born Private David MacKay for great personal gallantry in capturing one of the Colours of the 2nd Loodhiana Regiment after a desperate struggle. Later in the day Private MacKay was severely wounded during the fighting to capture the Shah Nujjiff. He was elected by the Private soldiers of the Regiment as one who had performed admirably during the attack. The second Victoria Cross of the engagement was awarded to Colour Sergeant James Munro from Cromarty, for his devoted gallantry at the Secundra Bagh in rescuing Captain Walsh also of the 93rd Highlanders who had been wounded and was in great danger where he was lying. The Colour Sergeant carried the officer to a place of comparative safety to which he was later brought himself after he had also been seriously wounded. The third award was made to Sergeant John Paton (fig.3) for his work in reconnoitring the next objective after the capture of the Secundra Bagh, the Shah Nujjiff. On his own initiative the Stirling born soldier went out under an extremely heavy fire and discovered a breach in the defences through which his Regiment was able to enter and capture this important position. The fourth Victoria Cross for the Regiment was won by Captain William George Drummond Stewart for his gallantry in leading the attack on two guns which resulted in the capture of the next fortified position, the Mess House. The action by the Perthshire born officer prevented much loss of life and secured the left flank of the attack on the Secundra Bagh. Captain Stewart's medal was awarded as a result of a ballot carried out by the commissioned officers of the Regiment. Captain Stewart was the son of Sir William Stewart the seventh Baronet of Grandtully in Perthshire. The other two Crosses won by the 93rd Highlanders were awarded to two Irishmen serving with the Regiment. The first of these was won by Lance Corporal John Dunlay for being the first man then surviving of the Regiment who had entered the very narrow breach through which the fort was eventually captured. The last award for the Regiment went to Private Peter Grant for his great personal gallantry in killing five of the enemy who had followed Lieutenant Colonel Ewart when he had captured the other Colour of the 2nd Loodhiana Regiment. Lieutenant Colonel Ewart was also recommended for the Victoria Cross but because Sir Colin Campbell did not wish to show favouritism to his Highlanders he decided that only one award was to be made to the officers of the 93rd and in the ballot Lieutenant Colonel Ewart lost out by 2 votes to Captain Stewart.

After the capture of the Secundra Bagh, which had taken most of the morning, the troops of Sir Colin's relieving column continued and cleared a village which was about 200 yards further on from their new now secure position. Led on by the old General himself the Highlanders then attacked the Shah Nujjiff through the breach which had been discovered by Sergeant Paton. After the storming parties had entered by the breach the fort was quickly captured and the Highlanders could rest knowing that they had done more than their share during the day.

The following day the defenders of the Residency on hearing the continued gunfire within earshot of them soon realised what was happening. Not long after the first meeting was arranged between the besieged Generals Havelock and Outram and the Commander in Chief in India, Sir Colin Campbell the ordeal for the defenders ended.

The wounded soldiers were sent as far back from the Residency as was safe in order that the Dhooli's, which were normally used as covered stretchers in a battle, could be used to evacuate the women and children from the Residency. The evacuation of the wounded, the women and children took three nights. This work was done entirely in the darkness so as to keep the enemy unaware of the plans to abandon the place.

Under cover of fire from the big Naval guns which had accompanied the relief column the last of the soldiers slipped away from the Residency not to return for another five months. The achievement of this cannot be underestimated as the total defending force did not exceed 4,000 men whilst the surrounding mutineers had more than 60,000 men in the town of Lucknow.

Two further Victoria Crosses were awarded to Glasgow men serving with the Bengal Artillery. In recognition of the part played by that Regiment in the days running up to the relief of the Residency they were asked to elect under clause 13 of the Royal Warrant of 29 January 1856, which allows officers and non commissioned soldiers to be selected to receive the decoration on behalf of the Regiment. Two of those selected were Gunners James Park and Hugh MacInnes for their part in the relief of Lucknow during the period 14 to 22 November 1857.

On 24 November the soldiers who had left Lucknow had established a new defensive position on the road to Cawnpore at a place known as the Alum Bagh. It was at this place that they buried Major General Havelock who had died of Dysentery. Sir Colin then left behind Sir James Outram's force in order that the road to Cawnpore could be kept open and an eye kept on Lucknow until the Commander in Chief could return with an army large enough to capture the town and hold it thereafter.

News of the relief of Lucknow spread throughout the army in India and to the troops who had still to embark for that country to quell the Mutiny. It was taken as a sign of the turning of the tide which was not to be stopped until peace returned once more.

Whilst away at Lucknow the situation at Cawnpore had deteriorated to the extent that the defenders there were on the point of again capitulating when Sir Colin's column returned at the end of the month and allowed the defenders there to be evacuated and sent to the safety of Allahabad. After the entry into Cawnpore the enemy forces which beforehand had been one of the better organised of the mutineers was in almost total disarray. This time of apparent lull in the fighting was used to build up the forces at the disposal of Sir Colin to prepare for an all out onslaught on Lucknow which had become on both sides a symbol of final victory, in that it was felt that the recapture would signify the nearing of the end for the Mutiny.

Meanwhile many small skirmishes were taking place throughout the Ganges Valley and it was during one of these encounters that Troop Sergeant Major David Spence, from Inverkeithing in Fife, serving in the 9th Lancers won his Victoria Cross. On 17 January 1858 the 9th Lancers as part of Brigadier General Hope Grant's Cavalry Brigade encountered a large party of mutineers at Shunsabad. In the heat of the action Sergeant Major Spence went out to the assistance of Private Kidd of the Lancers who had been wounded and was surrounded by a large band of rebels. The Scot immediately set about the rebels and was able to bring the wounded man back to safety.

By the middle of February an army, in greater numbers than that used in previous attempts at rescue was starting to assemble at the Alum Bagh for what was to prove to be the final assault on the rebel stronghold at Lucknow.

On the morning of 1 March 1858 Lanarkshire born Lieutenant Frederick Robertson Aikman commanding the 3rd Sikh Cavalry advanced with 100 of his men against a band of rebel infantry numbering about 500 men and completely routed them. In the action over 100 of the enemy were killed and two guns were captured. The survivors escaped by crossing the River Gumti onto ground which was difficult for the cavalry horses to move over. During the fighting the gallant Lieutenant received a severe sabre cut to the face as the result of his personal combat with several of the enemy. For his gallantry and leadership on this morning Lieutenant Aikman was recommended for and received the Victoria Cross.

On 2 March Sir Colin Campbell having gathered sufficient forces to recapture Lucknow marched out with support from both Cavalry and Artillery. In front of this great army the mutineers retreated as far as the Dilkhoosa Palace which they had fought over a few months previously. This new force almost 30,000 strong contained about 18,000 European troops and almost 200 guns. It was in fact the largest British army that had ever assembled in India to that date. This vast army now surrounded the town of Lucknow and had crossed the River Gumti and engaged the enemy within the very boundaries of the town. It was at this time that Lieutenant Francis Farquharson of the 42nd Regiment led a company of his men against a bastion containing two guns which were firing on positions captured in the fighting earlier on 9 March. The guns were spiked and the captured enemy emplacement was defended until the morning of 10 March. Whilst engaged in the defence of the bastion Lieutenant Farquharson was severely wounded. However the Glasgow born soldier recovered to receive his well deserved Victoria Cross.

As the fighting in and around Lucknow continued another Scots born soldier won the Victoria Cross. It was on 11 March at the Begum Bagh that Lieutenant and Adjutant of the 93rd Highlanders William McBean (fig.4), a ploughman's son from Inverness, led his men through the fort in pursuit of rebels. When he came across Lieutenant Grimston who had been set upon by a number of the enemy Lieutenant McBean immediately attacked them and after a short struggle lasting only 20 minutes he killed 11 of them with his own hands.

It was a further fortnight of bitter fighting in the narrow streets and lanes of Lucknow before the whole town was in British hands, never to be lost for the rest of the campaign. It was said that there was at least 100,000 mutineers in Lucknow and they were prepared to defend it to the last drop of blood. With the recapture of Lucknow the army remained for a few more days before it was split into a number of Field Forces which were to act independently of each other and in different parts of the rebel held provinces.

After the success at Lucknow the fighting moved towards Central India and it was at Betwah on 1 April that Aberdeenshire born Lieutenant James Leith won his Victoria Cross for having charged alone into a large number of rebel infantry to rescue a wounded Captain of his own Regiment, the 14th Light Dragoons.

Meanwhile on the same day Sir Hugh Rose who had brought a force from Indore in February was besieging the rebel held town of Jhansi when he was attacked by Tantia Topi who was considered as one of the mutineers greatest and most able leaders. A company of the 86th Regiment was ordered to remove a gun which was causing some damage to the attacking force. Without a moments hesitation Lieutenant and Adjutant Hugh Cochrane from Fort William dashed forward at a gallop and under a heavy fire directed entirely at him and drove the enemy from the gun emplacement. There he remained alone keeping the enemy at bay until the rest of his company arrived to assist him. At which point he continued the attack on the enemy rearguard. Although he was not wounded in the action he had three horses shot from under him in quick succession and survived to receive the Victoria Cross for his conspicuous gallantry throughout the day when the column was attacked by Tantia Topi. While Sir Hugh Rose was attacking rebels at every opportunity Sir Colin back at Lucknow was being a lot more cautious.

On 7 April 1858 a force under the command of Brigadier General Wauchope, containing a brigade of infantry made up from the 42nd, 79th and 93rd Regiments as well as a regiment of Native Infantry set out for the area known as the Rolikhand. This Rolikhand Field Force as it was to become known as set out from Lucknow in a north westerly direction. The vast majority of the soldiers were experiencing their first Indian summer as temperatures rose to over 120 degrees, which had a very debilitating effect on many of them. Without rest this column marched through the worst summer conditions the sub continent could muster and eventually reached the Fort at Ruhya which was found to be occupied by rebel soldiers. The attacking forces, led by the 42nd Regiment made their way closer to the fort through a thick wood. The attack was made with no preparation and as a result the infantry were cut to pieces despite a consistent barrage by the Artillery as they advanced on this rebel stronghold.

It was during this early part of the battle that Lieutenant Willoughby of the 4th Punjab Rifles was shot and killed. His body was lying exposed on top of the glacis of the fort when Captain Cafe, the Commanding Officer of the dead Lieutenant's Regiment called for volunteers to bring in his body. Private Edward Spence from Dumfries and Lance Corporal Alexander Thompson from Edinburgh stepped forward to assist the Captain. The three men went forward and located the body and as it was being borne away Private Spence exposed himself to the rebel fire in order to allow cover for the other two as they made their way back to safety. In doing so he was fatally wounded and died of his wounds on 17 April. For this action Captain Cafe of the 4th Punjab Rifles and Lance Corporal Thompson of the 42nd Regiment were both awarded the Victoria Cross. In the London Gazette of 27 May 1859 the awards to Thompson and Cafe were announced. As an addendum to the Gazette it was also announced that the award of the Victoria Cross would have been conferred on Private Spence had he survived the action. However on the 15 January 1907 there appeared in the London Gazette a list of confirmations of the award of the Victoria Cross to several soldiers who had died in actions which had they survived would have resulted in the medal. Amongst those named was Private Edward Spence of the 42nd Regiment who became the winner of the earliest posthumous Victoria Cross.

The 42nd Regiment won a third decoration at the attack on Fort Ruhya on 15 April when Edinburgh born Private James Davis carried back to the safety of the lines the body of another Lieutenant who had been killed on a forward reconnaissance to a gate of the fort.

The fourth Victoria Cross of the action was awarded to Quarter Master Sergeant John Simpson, who twice during the attack on the Fort went out under a very heavy and intensive fire and rescued from an exposed position within forty yards of the enemy parapet, a Lieutenant and Private who had both been severely wounded. Sergeant Simpson was born in Edinburgh on 29 June 1826 and died in Perth on 27 October 1883.

After the attack on the 15 April the Field Force fell back to await results and when nothing happened on 17 April the fort was entered without a shot being fired as the enemy had escaped during the night leaving behind the bodies of their dead. On entering the fort it was quickly realised that it had been in a poor state of defence and if a proper survey had been carried out before any attack had been launched there would not have been so many casualties in the initial attack.

As the heat of the summer increased it became more and more difficult for the Field Force to find any mutineers. As the final stages of the campaign were starting to fall into place the Highland Brigade, consisting of the 42nd, 78th, 79th and 93rd Highlanders marched on the rebel held town of Barielly. On 5 May the Highlanders attacked the town but because of the intense heat of the Indian summer the attack was suspended. During the attack Colour Sergeant William Gardner of the 42nd Regiment was awarded the Victoria Cross for having saved the life of his Commanding Officer Lieutenant Colonel Cameron, who had been knocked from his horse and was being attacked by three fanatical rebels. Colour sergeant who was born in Nemphlar in Lanarkshire without any hesitation ran out and bayonetted two of them and was in the process of killing the third when the rebel was shot by another soldier. The town was captured by the Highlanders the very next day.

As the summer wore on the hunt for rebels continued into the Gwalior Region and on 13 June at Nawabgunge the enemy were attacked by men of the 3rd Battalion of the Rifle Brigade. The riflemen had come across a force of mutineers formed up and ready for a fight. They were immediately attacked and during that attack the conduct of Private John Shaw was noted when an armed rebel was seen to enter a tope of trees and was at once followed by some men including Private Shaw. In the action which followed the Private drew his short sword and single handed rushed the Ghazee. Although he received a severe tulwar wound from the religious fanatic he eventually killed him after a fierce struggle. For this act of unselfish bravery Private Shaw from Prestonpans was rewarded with the Victoria Cross.

It was also during the rounding up of rebels in the Gwalior Region at Marar that Private George Rogers from Govan in Glasgow was awarded the Victoria Cross for daring conduct on 16 June in attacking alone a party of seven rebels. In the attack he dispersed them after he had killed one of them. This act of bravery took place while Private Rogers was in advance of his Regiment the 71st.

By the early days of January 1859 the Mutiny had been quashed although rebels were still being rounded. On 15 January at Maylah Ghat the dispatch of General Walpole records the conduct of two Private soldiers of the 42nd Regiment who at a time when the fighting was of a most severe nature and a few men of the 42nd Regiment were skirmishing so close to the enemy that they were receiving sword wounds. It was during this fighting that these two men went up to the front of the attack and began to direct the others of their company with courage and a coolness not normally expected of ordinary soldiers. These two Privates were Duncan Millar from Kilmarnock and Walter Cook from London and both of them survived to receive a well deserved Victoria Cross each.

By April 1859 the Mutiny was completely over and all parts affected by it had returned to normality, although for the British soldier serving in India life would never be the same.

During the whole 18 months of the campaign a total of 182 Victoria Crosses were gazetted 29 of which were won by Scottish born soldiers.

CHINA 1860

Since the late 1830's the Chinese Government had been at loggerheads with the British over the question of the importation of opium into China. The Chinese were not at all happy with what was a British monopoly of a very profitable business and tried to impose a ban. In January 1839 the Chinese in Canton overran warehouses operated by British merchants and destroyed vast quantities of opium. Thus began what was to be known as "the Opium Wars" which resulted in Britain sending Her troops to take control of the parts of the Chinese Empire which were largely populated by Europeans. By 1842 peace had been restored and conditions for the European traders had returned to near normality. However by 1856 the mistreating of the Europeans living in the Empire had increased to a dangerous level so much so that when a Chinese ship sailing under the British flag was boarded and most of the crew taken off the British Commander in China Admiral Sir Michael Seymour demanded an apology from the Chinese.

When there was no response to his demands he immediately attacked and captured the Chinese port of Canton with the rather small force at his disposal then. As he did not have enough of a force to maintain his advantage he called for reinforcements from India. When they arrived he commenced the operations against the Chinese, however as the momentum of the Indian Mutiny had increased by the summer of 1857 Regiments such as the 93rd Highlanders which had originally been destined for China were diverted.

By December 1857 reinforcements had arrived in sufficient numbers to allow the operations against the enemy to restart with a greater intensity. Realising the seriousness of Britain's intentions the Chinese Government sued for peace in January 1859 and Britain was in agreement as long as the any peace treaty was signed in the Chinese capital Peking. When the Envoys arrived to pave the way for peace they found that there was not a decrease in the Chinese hostility towards them.

Throughout this time the Taku Forts on either side of the River Peiho were proving to be a major stumbling block to any advance up river to the Chinese capital. In June 1859 a mainly Naval force under the command of Admiral Sir James Hope, who had succeeded Admiral Seymour, attacked the forts in an effort to force a way through to Peking for the newly appointed British Ambassador Sir Frederick Bruce. This attack proved unsuccessful and the Fleet with the Ambassador on board had to withdraw. It was then decided upon a joint effort between Britain and France. The British force was commanded by Lieutenant General Sir James Hope Grant, a Scots born soldier who had greatly distinguished himself during the Indian Mutiny. On 21 August 1860 the British numbering some 13,000 men attacked both the north and south Taku Forts which ever since the attack by Admiral Hope had stood defiantly in the way of any missions to Peking.

It was during the attack on the northern fort on the River Peiho that a young twenty year old Private from Edinburgh named John McDougall of the 44th Regiment displayed great gallantry after he had swum the water filled ditch which was surrounding the fort. This was carried out with an Officer of his own Regiment, Lieutenant Robert Rogers, and another officer from the 67th Regiment. After they had crossed the ditch all three continued to fight their way into the fort and were the first British soldiers to enter into the fort. Later on in the day both forts had been captured. For his actions throughout the attack on the north Taku Fort Private McDougall was awarded one of the eight Victoria Crosses won during the whole campaign to suppress the Chinese. Seven of these medals were won for gallantry during the attack on the Taku forts on 21 August 1860.

The war in China ended on 13 October 1860 when the victorious British troops entered Peking.

NEW ZEALAND 1864

Ever since the discovery of New Zealand by Abel Tasman in 1642 it was always thought of as being an ideal place for the British as it resembled Britain in so many aspects with the additional advantage of improvement in the weather. Almost 250 years later the native peoples of the Islands, the Maoris, were beginning to realise what was happening to them and their lands. In 1845 the Maori Chiefs in both the North and South Islands rebelled against this not very subtle infiltration. Although this first Native rebellion had been quelled in the whole of New Zealand by 1847 the unrest continued almost continually for the next 30 years.

After a relatively quiet spell from 1861 to 1863 renewed fighting broke out in May 1863 and spread quickly throughout the colony. The British garrison was reinforced by fresh troops from Britain and Australia. The delay in sending sufficient troops to suppress the Maoris allowed them to erect a strongly fortified position at Pukehinahina called the Gate Pah, which barred the way for any attacks against the natives.

On 30 March 1864 near Ohanpu in the North Island Lieutenant Colonel John Carstairs McNeill (fig.5), the Aide de Campe of Lieutenant General Sir Duncan Cameron, was carrying despatches to the town of Te Awamutu when he was attacked by a band of about 50 Maoris. Lieutenant Colonel McNeill was accompanied by two Privates of the Colonial Defence Force. When the three men were attacked Lieutenant Colonel McNeill immediately sent back one of the Privates, Gibson by name, to bring infantry support. In the action which followed his remaining companion Private Vosper was dislodged from his horse after it had stumbled. On seeing this the Lieutenant Colonel returned to the soldier who by this time was surrounded by natives and caught up his horse and allowed him to remount. After which they had to fight their way through the enemy to make good their escape without further injury.

As a result of his unselfishness on that day the Officer who had been born on the tiny west coast island of Colonsay and was eventually to become the Laird of it, received a well deserved Victoria Cross.

In April 1864 an attack was made against the Gate Pah which resulted in many casualties for the attackers. Although the war had been won after this attack it was continued into the bush and British soldiers were involved in the bush war until the summer of 1866.

Of all the fifteen Victoria Crosses won in the Maori Wars Lieutenant Colonel McNeill's was the only one won by a Scottish born soldier.

INDIA 1865/72

Since the mid 1850's British and Indian army troops had been involved in skirmishes with various hill tribes in India's northern mountains. In the Bhootan area the local tribes had carried on a virtual continuous harassment into neighbouring British held territory. This culminated in the rebuttal by the tribesmen of a Diplomatic Mission sent into the territory to negotiate for an end to the continual raids into the British held territory. After such an insult on Her Majesty's representative the Indian Government decided to send in troops to put the tribesmen of Bhootan in their place. Although there were some small actions in and around some enemy held towns the tribesmen were apparently ready for peace after the show of strength by the British.

Even after this the attacks on British garrisons restarted and a force under the command of Brigadier General Sir Henry Tombs, who had won a Victoria Cross as a Major during the siege of Delhi in 1857, was sent into the area to suppress the tribesmen. At the battle fought around the town of Dewangiri on 30 April 1865 Sir Henry Tombs' column met and defeated a force of Bhootanies. During the fighting for the town the General ordered two Officers to climb the wall of a loopholed house which was being so desperately defended that it was holding up the capture of the town. The two Officers of the Bengal Engineers Lieutenant James Dundas, who had been born in Edinburgh, and Major William Trevor had to climb almost fifteen foot of wall and then enter the building head first through one of the loopholes. Once in the two men held the defenders at bay until reinforcements could arrive by the same route. In the close quarter fight both Officers were wounded and both recovered to receive the Victoria Crosses which had been awarded to them.

The conflict in Bhootan was not ended until 1866 when a further column was mounted to bring their warlike activities to a halt.

The operations against the hill tribes continued for many more years and in 1871 the daughter of a British tea planter was kidnapped by some tribesmen from the area of Looshai. In response to this kidnapping two columns of Native troops were sent into the region to rescue the young Englishwoman. The plan consisted of attacking a Looshai held village and then searching for Miss Winchester, the planters daughter. During one of these searches Major Donald MacIntyre, who was born in Kincraig in the Scottish Highlands, and was serving with the Bengal Staff Corps attached to the 2nd Gurkha Rifles, led the assault on the fortified Looshai village of Lalgnoora. Accompanied by soldiers of the 2nd Gurkha's he was the first to reach the walls of the stockade which at that point were over nine feet high. The stockade was successfully stormed by this Officer even after the heaviest fire of the day had been directed at him. For his gallantry on 4 January 1872 at the village of Lalgnoora Major MacIntyre was awarded the Victoria Cross.

Eventually the Looshai tribesmen agreed upon terms for peace and released Miss Winchester after three months in captivity.

In India during these seven years a total of only three Victoria Crosses were awarded and two of these were won by Lieutenant Dundas and Major MacIntyre.

ASHANTI 1873/74

The main cause of the disturbance in Ashanti was that in 1872 the main port of the West African kingdom, Elmina, was transferred from Dutch to British control and thus ended the annual payments made by Holland to King Kofi Karikara for the use of the port. Angered by this the King of Ashanti sent his troops across the border and attacked the friendly tribes in the British Protectorate of the Gold Coast. At this time there were only a few British troops in the Gold Coast and reinforcement had to be sent under the command of Sir Garnet Wolseley. Shortly after the arrival of the additional forces the Ashantis were defeated at the battles of Essaman and Escaber. By the beginning of January 1874 the British had begun the advance on the Ashanti capital of Coomassie. During this advance many small difficult actions were fought. The conditions under which these actions were fought were typified at the battle in the dense bush around the Ashanti town of Amoaful. It was at this battle that the men of the 42nd Highlanders distinguished themselves by being at the forefront of the attack. None was more distinguished in the battle than Lance Sergeant Samuel McGaw (fig.6) who although severely wounded early on in the attack led his section through the dense thorny bush and engaged the enemy several times throughout the day. For his gallant conduct throughout the battle, considering he had been wounded, the soldier who was born in Kirkmichael in Ayrshire was awarded the Victoria Cross, one of only Four men to receive it for the campaign in Ashanti.

In the following month King Karikara realising that he had no hope against the might of Britain agreed to sign a peace treaty which ended yet another small war for Her Majesty Queen Victoria.

AFGHANISTAN 1878/79

The war in the hills of Afghanistan in 1878 was the second major campaign in which British troops had been involved in a little more than 40 years. The country had long been considered as a buffer between the ambitions of two of the most powerful nations in the world in the 19th Century, Britain and Russia. The Amir of Afghanistan Shere Ali, after a series of disputes with the British Government, decided to ratify a treaty with Russia which would allow Britains arch enemy access to Afghanistan for the purpose of protection. This move by the Amir upset the delicate balance in the region and Britain felt obliged to send an ultimatum to Shere Ali in October 1878. When no reply had been received by the due date three columns were sent across the border into Afghanistan on the following day, 21 November.

One of these columns which came to be known as the Kuru Valley Field Force moved across the border and almost immediately attacked the Afghans at Peiwar-Kotal which guarded the main route through the valleys to the Afghan capital Kabul. The enemy had taken time to fortify the town in anticipation of the advance of the Force which was commanded by Major General Frederick Roberts, who was yet another of these Victorian Generals who had risen through the ranks after having won a Victoria Cross in India in January 1858.

On the morning of 2 December, whilst the attackers were in the trenches before the town, an assault was initiated by Edinburgh born, Captain John Cook of the Bengal Staff Corps, and attached to the 5th Gurkha Rifles. He rushed out of the trenches with such determination that the enemy fled from the field. During the confusion which followed the Edinburgh born officer noticed a Major of his own Corps engaged in single combat with an Afghan warrior. Captain Cook distracted the attention of the Afghan and continued with the struggle from his exhausted fellow officer. In the close combat both men fell to the ground and the native immediately sunk his teeth into the arm of Captain Cook releasing his grip after a single shot had been fired into his head. For his dash and gallantry on that day Captain Cook was decorated with the Victoria Cross. He was however destined not to wear his medal for very long as he was killed in action at Sherpur a year later.

After the defeat at Peiwar-Kotal, Shere Ali escaped from Kabul and did not take further part in the war, however his son Yakub Khan took command and continued the fight against the British until 30 May 1879 when peace was again restored.

As a result of the victory at Peiwar-Kotal, British troops were established in the Khyber Pass. The peace was again broken in September 1879 when many of the British residents in Kabul were murdered. When word of this massacre reached the British Government General Roberts was ordered to march on Kabul to restore peace. Having entered Kabul he immediately set about strengthening the defences and concentrating his forces at the Sherpur Pass which protected the main route to the city. The fighting around the city continued for another 14 days. During one of the many attacks on the British defences Lieutenant William Dick-Cunyngham of the Gordon Highlanders saw that the defence was faltering after having been forced back onto the top of a hill exposed himself to the full fury of the enemy guns to rally his men. By his example and calling on those behind him to follow he charged into the main body of the enemy and saved the position from being overrun. For his leadership and gallant conduct on 13 December Lieutenant Dick-Cunyngham, who was born at Prestonfield in Edinburgh was rewarded with the Victoria Cross.

The following day in the defences around Kabul two more Scottish born soldiers were awarded the Victoria Cross. The first of these was won by Lance Corporal George Sellar from Keith who was serving with the Seaforth Highlanders in the hills around the Afghan capital. From their positions in the Asmai Heights the gallant Seaforths were under constant fire from the Afghan gunners. Whilst leading an attack on the enemy positions Lance Corporal Sellar was the first to reach and engage the enemy with his rifle and bayonet. In the fighting this brave Scot was wounded by an Afghan wielding a knife. Whilst he was involved in the attack the whole episode was being watched by General Roberts through a telescope and he had no hesitation in awarding an immediate Victoria Cross to the brave Lance Corporal.

The second Cross of the day was won by Captain William Vousden of the Bengal Staff Corps who was attached to the 5th Punjab Cavalry. During the attack on the Asmai Heights Captain Vousden charged with a small party of his cavalry into the centre of a line of Afghans who were more intent on retreating than fighting. Although outnumbered this small band of horsemen continued to fight backwards and forwards through the enemy. For his gallantry and leadership the Perth born officer was awarded Scotlands second Victoria Cross of the day.

The war continued until late 1880 General Roberts made his now famous march over 22 days in August from the capital Kabul to Kandahar, where he defeated the other son of Shere Ali, Ayub Khan, at the Battle of Kandahar and brought peace to the area yet again.

In the campaign in Afghanistan a total of 16 Victoria Crosses were won of which no less than 4 were awarded to Scottish born soldiers.

INDIA 1891/97

Lord Roberts in his book "Forty-one Years in India" describes Manipur as "a petty state on the confines of Assam" and it was here that the next Victoria Cross was won by a Scot. Internal disputes in Manipur had resulted in the British Government trying to bring about the overthrow of the ruler of that petty state because confidence had been lost in him. British troops were sent into the area and after they had been duped by the promise of talks, Colonel Skene and the Chief Commissioner for Assam, Mr J W Quinton, went to the headquarters of the Manipuris and were never seen again. As a direct result of this fresh fighting broke out and the British had to withdraw. After the disastrous events at Manipur, Lieutenant Charles Grant (fig.33) of the Indian Staff Corps, volunteered to lead an expedition to try and rescue the British captives. On the 21 March 1891 with a small force of about 80 men he was able to capture the town of Thobal which was close to Manipur. For nearly three weeks the would be rescuers held the town against overwhelming odds. For his inspiration and daring during this time, this officer, who was born in Bourtie in Aberdeenshire was awarded the only Victoria Cross of this disastrous episode in India.

The troubles in the Indian Frontier region continued for several more years. The next Scot to win a Victoria Cross was Piper George Findlater of the 1st Battalion of the Gordon Highlanders. By October 1897 the troubles in India had moved to the Tirah Region. The Government was taking no chances and the Tirah Expeditionary Force exceeded 30,000 men. The main and decisive action of the campaign was fought over three days at the village of Dargai. The battle for the village had begun on 18 October and was very indecisive. Two days later the decision was taken to storm the village at all costs. The first part of the final assault was carried out by men of the Gurkha Rifles and the Dorset and Devon Regiments. By the afternoon it was being reported that the storming of the Dargai Heights could only be successful if a great loss of life was acceptable. At this point in the battle the Gordon Highlanders were ordered to take the hill at all costs. When the bugles sounded and the pipes played the men of the Gordons moved off with bayonets fixed. The enemy then fled when confronted with the Gordons advancing tipped with steel. The final assault on the Heights did not waver for one moment and much of the credit must go to Piper Findlater who although he had been shot through both legs propped himself up against a rock and continued to play the Regimental tunes of glory. For his devotion to his battlefield job on the day of the storming of the Dargai Heights Piper Findlater, who was born at Forgue near Huntly in Aberdeenshire, was presented with his Victoria Cross by Her Majesty Queen Victoria in the hospital bed where he was recuperating from his wounds.

In the final storming of the heights at Dargai four Victoria Crosses were won and two of these were won by men of the Gordon Highlanders.

RHODESIA 1896

In 1896, the year after the country had been given its new name, some of the indigenous peoples revolted and set about massacring white people who were seen as the symbols of the new Rhodesia. The rebels concentrated their murders on policemen and native commissioners. By mid March of 1896 two Forces had taken to the field to relieve the situation. One of these, the Bulawayo Field Force was operating in and around the Rhodesian capital. A patrol had gone out into the bush to a place called Campbell's Store and had become encircled by the Matabeles under their leader Chief Olimo. On 30 March another patrol was sent out to try and rescue those surrounded at Campbell's Store. Amongst the rescuers was Trooper Herbert Henderson who had moved to Rhodesia in 1894 after he had emigrated to the Rand in 1892 from Hillhead in Glasgow. In the fight which had taken place Trooper Henderson and a companion who had been wounded in the knee when his horse had been killed under him found themselves alone. Although both men were cut off from the main party the Glasgow man mounted the wounded man Trooper Celliers on his horse and made good their escape from the natives. Because of the danger in the countryside, Herbert Henderson was only able to travel at night and walked the full 35 miles back to Bulawayo where his wounded comrade was treated. This remarkable journey through the rebel held countryside took two days and one night. For his courage during this time, which was carried out without food, the Glasgow born volunteer in the fight in his new country was awarded one of the three Victoria Crosses gazetted for the campaign in Matabeleland.

ASHANTI 1900

The general situation in the west of Africa was one of uneasy peace which erupted into open rebellion by the natives of Ashanti in March 1900. The capital of that country was immediately encircled and this caused many to die through disease and starvation. As the situation at Coomassie deteriorated it became of utmost importance that the numbers of non-combatants in the capital should be reduced. When the civilians had been evacuated there was only a garrison of a few men left. It was at this time that Sergeant John MacKenzie of the 2nd Battalion of the Seaforth Highlanders, who was employed in the West Africa Field Force displayed the greatest gallantry in volunteering to clear an enemy stockade. He led the charge himself and chased the enemy into the bush. He still had the energy to do this even after he had been working two Maxim guns for most of the day until he was wounded. For his gallantry and leadership at Dompoassi on 6 June 1900 the Sergeant, who was born in Contin in Ross-shire, was decorated with one of the two Victoria Crosses won during the campaign in Ashanti.

SOUTH AFRICA 1899/1902

In May 1902 the Treaty of Vereeniging was signed and thus ended three years of embarrassment for the British soldiers who had fought what was to become known as the Great Boer War. The might of Britain and her Empire had dared to tackle the lowly farmers of South Africa. These farmers originally from the Dutch who had colonised this part of Africa in the late 17th century. By the end of the 18th century these Boers as they had become known had developed a culture that made them unique in African terms. The defeat of Napoleon Bonaparte in 1815 and the division of France's colonies resulted in the Cape Colony becoming British. As much as this suited the British it did not please the Boers in the slightest. As every Government was interested in the coast of South Africa and nobody was interested in the interior the Boers took advantage of the situation and moved inland. Throughout the early part of the 19th century the Boers had tried to resist the British rule. Finally in 1836 they began what they called the Great Trek and totally dissatisfied with British domination, and more especially Britain's attitude towards slavery, they set out in small groups from the Cape Colony across the Orange River. Once across they named their new country the Orange Free State. Britain fearful for the safety of her own people in Southern Africa and felt the need to annex in 1843 Natal, the Homeland of the Zulu nation and a few Boer trekkers.

Halfway through the century Britain was not keen to become involved in further annexations in South Africa and in 1852 the new Boer states of Orange Free State and the Transvaal were recognised. This move gave the area peace for the next twenty years. However in 1870 diamonds were discovered in the area around Kimberley in the tribal lands west of the Orange Free State, known as Griqualand West. In 1871 the tribal Chief anxious for his own safety from across the border sought the help of the British Government and in the same year the tribal lands were annexed by agreement. This effectively prevented Boer expansion westwards.

By their attitude towards the Zulus, the Boers were causing unrest in other parts of South Africa. In 1877 under the pretence of financial rescue Britain finally annexed the bankrupt state of Transvaal in order to prevent Zulu expansion in the interior. At this time in history the Boers were too weak to have resisted any invasion by the Zulu nation. Although this prevented invasion it did not prevent the Zulus trying to settle old scores in the area. These long-standing quarrels caused Britain to go to war against them in 1879. While the British were celebrating the heroic stand at Rorke's Drift the Boers were more interested in the massive defeat of British troops at Isandhlwana. This to the Boers had shown the British to be weak and seizing their chance sought independence which had been promised at the time of the annexation. Although the British Prime Minister at the time William Ewart Gladstone was sympathetic to the Boer cause the Government was slow to make up its mind on the question of independence. In 1881 the Boers again took up arms against Britain and inflicted a humiliating defeat on her forces on 26 February 1881 at Majuba Hill. (A defeat which was to remain long in the memories of British soldiers serving in South Africa.) Undeterred or even frightened by the defeat of her army in Africa the Prime Minister still sympathetic to the Boer cause granted Independence by signing the Convention of Pretoria in 1881.

Peace returned to the area for another short time and in 1886 when gold was discovered in the Witwatersrand, south of Pretoria tensions mounted caused by the influx of foreigners into the area in search of their fortunes. These foreigners termed "Uitlanders" by the Boers suffered under a very unfair tax system used by the Boer Government to meet its responsibilities.

In late December 1895 these "Uitlanders" plotted to overthrow the Boer Government and led by Doctor Jamieson, the Administrator of Rhodesia, they crossed over the border into the Transvaal. However their intentions were conveyed to the Boers and they were met at Krugersdorp and heavily defeated. The leaders were captured and put on trial in London. To the rest of the world this raid seemed to have been carried out with the knowledge of the British Government and to the British it was most embarrassing.

The "Uitlanders" in the Transvaal continued to seek rights from the Boers and Britain again tried to interfere in Boer internal affairs. President Kruger in Pretoria frustrated by this intervention sent an ultimatum to the British demanding that all troops be removed from the borders of the Transvaal otherwise war would be declared. The Boers apart from underestimating the strength of the British were also expecting help from the Germans which never came.

On 12 October 1899 war was declared and so began the second war against the Boer farmers. With the declaration of war the Boers of the Orange Free State joined with the Boers in Transvaal and crossed the borders into Natal and the Cape Colony. Once across the borders they immediately moved to all points of the compass and engaged the numerically inferior British forces and began to besiege the towns of Mafeking, Kimberley and Ladysmith. At this early stage of the conflict all did not look good for Britain and her position as mistress of South Africa looked to be coming to an end. However this conflict so far from Britain aroused more feelings of patriotism throughout the Empire than any of the war which Britain had fought during the already long reign of Queen Victoria.

The early attempts by the British at counter attack met with success and at the Battle of Talana fought on 20 October 1899 the hopes of an early defeat for the Boers were renewed. This was reinforced a day later on the banks of the Sunday River at Elandslaagte when in the midst of a great thunderstorm the British were attacked by Boer forces. Amidst the shells and the rain the men of the 2nd Battalion of the Gordon Highlanders commanded by Lieutenant Colonel Dick-Cunyngham who had won a Victoria Cross in Afghanistan twenty years earlier, threw themselves into the charge with all the dash and courage which had been traditionally expected from the men from the Highlands of Scotland. The speed of the advance against men fighting in the kind of ground in which they had always lived inevitably caused many casualties amongst the Gordons. It was during these advances in the final stages of the battle that, Dumfries born Sergeant Major William Robertson, led each of the charges against the enemy positions. In order to encourage his men he exposed himself to the very accurate fire from the Boers. After the ground had been won he led a small party of the Highlanders and captured the remains of the Boer camp, which was held in spite of repeated counter attacks from the enemy. It was during one of these counter attacks that the gallant Sergeant Major was wounded and had to be returned to the rear. For his courage and outstanding leadership on that day he was decorated with the Victoria Cross, one of only four awarded for action during the Battle of Elandslaagte.

After these early successes by the British the Boers began to realise that in order to defeat them they had to fight as they knew not in the ordered form of the British Army. In December of that year the news of defeats for the British were being announced so frequently that the week in December came to be known as "Black Week". The setbacks at Modder River, Stromberg, Magersfontein and finally Colenso all served to boost the morale of the Boer.

On 15 December at Colenso, near Ladysmith, when the British Artillery had been formed up as if in ceremonial order the Boer gunners were able to take full advantage in spite of their lack of experience in long range bombardment. So much so that the practised British were forced to abandon some of their artillery pieces to the enemy. In this final action of "Black Week" there was a total of 7 Victoria Crosses won, 6 of them for various attempts to save the guns from being captured by the Boers. The seventh was awarded to Dumbarton born Major William Babtie (fig.37) of the Royal Army Medical Corps for his courage in attending to the many wounded from the action and more especially those men who had gallantly attempted the rescue of the guns. At the height of the bombardment Major Babtie rode out to attend to the many wounded who were lying in a donga close to the rear of the abandoned guns. In the course of carrying out his medical work he had to move several times during the day as Boer marksmen were giving him more than a fair bit of attention. Later in the day he and a fellow officer again went out to the rescue of Lieutenant the Honourable Frederick Roberts the only son of Lord Roberts who was to be appointed Commander in Chief after General Buller was relieved of his command after the disasters of that second week in December 1899. Lieutenant Roberts in spite of the valiant efforts of Major Babtie died later of the wounds he had received trying to rescue the guns and like the brave Scottish medical officer he also received the Victoria Cross just as his father had done over forty years previously.

The guns, over which so much blood was spilt and so much courage wasted, were eventually abandoned to the Boers before the day was done.

Once into the new century the Boers, who up to then had been fairly laid back in their siege of Ladysmith, decided to go onto the offensive and on 6 January Boer General Joubert led almost 5,000 men against the defences around the town. Under the guise of smaller diversionary attacks around the defences the main thrust came against a ridge known to the British at Ladysmith as Waggon Hill. Taking full advantage of the element of surprise the Boers quickly gained the supremacy of the ridge. However a small force of defenders led by Lieutenant Robert Digby-Jones of the Royal Engineers re-occupied the summit at a critical moment just as the leading Boer attackers were establishing themselves in the recently gained position. Lieutenant Jones and Trooper Albrecht of the Imperial Light Horse were the first to reach the top of the hill and both men immediately engaged the enemy. The Boer leader was shot by Jones and the other two men were shot by the Trooper. There is no doubt that but for the bravery of these two men the advantage of the hill would have been lost to the enemy. Later in the day in the defence of this hard won position the Lieutenant from Edinburgh was shot and killed. For the courage and leadership displayed by Lieutenant Digby-Jones during the defence of Waggon Hill he along with Trooper Albrecht was awarded the first gazetted posthumous Victoria Cross to go to a Scots born soldier.

By March 1900 General Roberts who was still grieving for his only son had captured the Orange Free State and had also managed to persuade many of the Boer farmers to return to their families. However he did not manage to persuade the leaders to do likewise. Throughout South Africa many Boers were beginning to realise that they could not win the war. For all those who had lost heart for the fight there were still many thousands scattered throughout the country who were of an even firmer belief that the war could be won. The conflict changed from one of almost set piece battles to one of what could be considered as individual fights. Believing that the Boers would be defeated if their Government fell the British concentrated their efforts in the areas of Johannesburg and Pretoria.

The vast British army as it moved towards Johannesburg had its spirits raised when word came that Mafeking had been relieved. As the army approached, the Gordon Highlanders were engaging the enemy around the town of Doornkop. On 20 May, on Crow's Nest Hill, Lance Corporal John MacKay serving in the 1st Battalion of the Gordons distinguished himself throughout the day by his efforts to attend to wounded men who were lying out in the open only a short distance from the enemy rifle positions. All this was carried out whilst he was constantly being fired upon by the enemy marksmen. Later in the day he went out alone into the open and carried a wounded man on his shoulders to the relative safety of a large boulder where he was able to tend the man's wounds. For his actions on this day Lance Corporal MacKay became the second Edinburgh born soldier to be decorated with the Victoria Cross.

On 4 June the Capital of the state of Transvaal was entered and fittingly the Gordon Highlanders were the first British soldiers to enter the town. After consolidating his position in the Boer capital General Roberts decided to make for Krugersdorp, the place where the Jamieson Raid had come to an end in 1896. On 11 July as his men advanced on the town of Leekoehoek they immediately came under an accurate fire from the Boer guns in the surrounding hills. The Artillery in their anxiety to defeat the Boers had advanced far ahead of the main army and in the fighting which followed were forced to again abandon guns to the enemy. After the order to withdraw and leave the guns had been given it was decided that an attempt to save them would be made. Captain David Younger from Edinburgh led out a small party of men from his Regiment, The Gordon Highlanders, and was successful in dragging under cover an artillery ammunition waggon. When this had been completed Captain William Gordon, also of the 1st Battalion of the Gordon Highlanders, went out alone to one of the abandoned guns and attached a rope with which to drag the gun to the safety of a nearby Kopje. He then called for volunteers and Captain Younger with 10 men came to his aid. At this point the small force were confronted by a very concentrated fire by which the enemy hoped to deter the men from their task of removing the gun. Four of the rescue party were wounded, including the gallant Captain Younger, who died shortly afterwards. Realising that it would be impossible to move the gun without further casualties Captain Gordon ordered those remaining unwounded to return to the safety of the Kopje to where they had intended to take the gun. He only retired to the safety after he had personally seen that all the wounded had reached cover. Later in the day he returned to the gun with Lance Corporal MacKay, who had earlier won the Victoria Cross at Doornkop and recovered the body of his gallant comrade Captain Younger.

It was not for the first time in the war in South Africa that men had performed most gallantly attempting to recover guns which had been abandoned to the enemy and as before the Victoria Cross was bestowed of these officers, Captain Younger and Captain Gordon, who had so valiantly organised the attempts to save the guns. Unfortunately the award to Captain Younger was one of the first posthumously gazetted.

With the annexation of the Transvaal and the announcement that the war was to all intents and purposes over, coupled with the appointment of Lord Kitchener of Khartoum as the new Commander in Chief led to new hope for an early peace in Africa. However even before Lord Roberts had left to return to Britain to be hailed as the hero against the Boers it became obvious that the spirit of the Boers had not yet been broken. The attempts to outfight the British by methods which had been practically invented by them were replaced by a type of warfare to which the Boer was best suited and his guerrilla war was to continue until peace was declared in 1902.

On 22 November 1900 at Dewetsdorp near Bloemfontein on one of the outposts known as Gibraltar Hill, Edinburgh born Private Charles Kennedy of the 2nd Battalion of the Highland Light Infantry was awarded a Victoria Cross for his determination and gallantry in carrying a wounded comrade over $^3/_4$ of a mile to hospital. This was carried out under a continuous rifle fire directed towards him by the enemy. On the following day he volunteered to act as a runner to carry a message from his Commanding Officer to the Commandant. The route across open ground was swept by enemy fire and meant almost certain death. However before he had gone but a few yards he was severely wounded and took no further part in the action.

After the fall of Pretoria and the annexation of the Transvaal, the Infantry were deployed mainly as mounted escorts to defend the many convoys of bullock wagons transporting stores, food and ammunition around the countryside. It was in one of these mounted columns that Sergeant Donald Farmer of the 1st Battalion of the Queen's Own Cameron Highlanders found himself on 13 December 1900 at General Clement's camp at Nooitgadacht near Pretoria. During an attack on the camp a Lieutenant and 15 men including Sergeant Farmer went to the aid of an advanced picquet which was being engaged by Boer riflemen. Most of the picquet had been wounded or killed and as the rescue party approached the enemy hidden in some trees they opened fire at a very close range and immediately killed 2 men and wounded 3 others including Lieutenant Sandilands. Sergeant Farmer immediately left his cover and under a heavy and attentive fire from the Boers carried the wounded officer to a place of comparative safety. Having secured the officer the Sergeant then returned to the firing line only to be captured by the enemy. After being held for a couple of days and fed with their own rations, the remainder of the Highlanders were sent on their way back to the British lines to resume the fight against the Boers.

For his actions of that day and in particular for his rescue of Lieutenant Sandilands, Kelso born Sergeant Farmer, won the first Victoria Cross to be awarded to a soldier of the Queen's Own Cameron Highlanders and which was the last award to be made to a Scottish born soldier in the Boer War.

Although no more Victoria Crosses were won by the Scottish troops played an important role in the operations through which it was hoped would bring this war, which had become an embarrassment, to Britain and her Empire to an early end. This was not to be and it raged on until the Treaty of Vereeniging was signed on 31 May 1902.

During the war a total of 78 Victoria Crosses were awarded of which 8 were won by Scottish born soldiers. The announcement of the awards in the London Gazette heralded the first Victoria Crosses to be conferred on soldiers from South Africa, Australia, Canada, and New Zealand as well as the first posthumous awards, 2 of which were awarded to Scots.

1. Lts. Malcolmson and Moore lead the charge of the 3rd Bombay Cavalry at Khooshab, February 1857.

2. Lt. William Rennie

3. Sgt. John Paton

4. Lt. William McBean

5. Lt. Col. John C. McNeill

6. L/Sgt. Samuel McGraw

7. Pte. Henry May

8. Cmdr. Henry P. Ritchie

9. Pte. Charles Melvin

*10.*Pte. Robert R. Dunsire

11. L/cpl. Samuel Frickleton

12. CSM. John Skinner

13. 2nd Lt. John C. Buchan

14. Sgt. John Meikle

15. Pte. Hugh McIver

16. T/Lt. David L. MacIntyre

17. Sgt. Louis McGuffie

18. Sgt. John Hannah

19. FO. Kenneth Campbell

20. T/Lt. Col. Geoffrey C.T. Keyes

21. A/Bi.g. John C. Campbell

22. CMDR. Anthony C.C. Miers

23. W/Cmdr. Hugh G. Malcolm

24. T/Ltd. Col. Lorne M. Campbell

25. Lt. Donald Campbell

26. A/Flt. Lt. William Reid

27. FO. John A. Cruickshank

28. Fl/Sgt. George Thompson

29. Pte. James Stokes

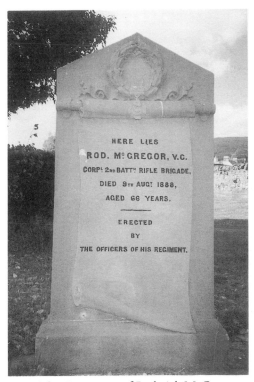

30. The Gravestone of Roderick McGregor.

VICTORIA CROSS

THE NEW ORDER OF VALOUR

FOR THE ARMY.

JOHN BERRYMAN, (TROOP SERG. MAJOR.) REFUSING TO LEAVE CAPTAIN WEBB AT BALAKLAVA.

W. NORMAN, (PRIVATE,) BRINGING IN SINGLE-HANDED TWO RUSSIAN PRISONERS.

JOHN GRIEVE (SERG. MAJOR) SAVING THE LIFE OF AN OFFICER AT BALAKLAVA.

THOMAS BEACH (PRIVATE.) AT INKERMAN, RESCUING COLONEL CARPENTER.

C. H. LUMLEY, BREVET MAJOR) IN THE REDAN, ENGAGED WITH THREE RUSSIAN GUNNERS.

F. C. ELTON (MAJOR) WORKING IN THE TRENCHES UNDER A HEAVY FIRE.

HONOUR TO THE BRAVE

31. The New Heroes

32. Lt. Robert Lindsay
V.C.

John Player

VC CARDS

33. Lt. Charles Grant
V.C.

Ogdens

34. F/O Kenneth Campbell V.C.

Bassett & Co.

35. Lt. Walter Brodie
V.C.M.C.

W.D. & H.O. Wills

36. Pte. David Lauder
V.C.

Gallaher

37. A selection of cards for Major William Babtie V.C.

38. Piper Findlater

39. Memorial to Sgt. John Meikle at Dingwall Station

40. Heroes for our Youth

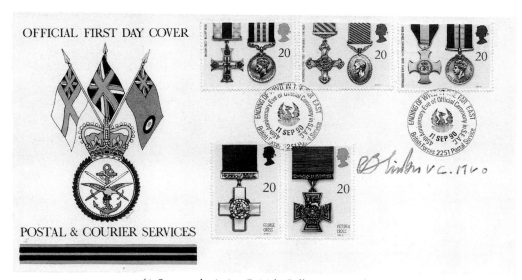

41. Stamps depicting British Gallantry Awards
Signed by L/Cpl. R. Limbu

42. The Last of Scotlands FORgotten Valour
Bill Reid, John Cruickshank with Michael Aspel.

CHAPTER 3

TWENTIETH CENTURY'S HEROES

THE GREAT WAR 1914/1919

On the afternoon of Sunday 28 June 1914, Europe and the rest of the World took that final step towards the greatest waste of manhood the World has ever known. On this day Archduke Franz Ferdinand of Austria and his wife Sophie arrived in Sarajevo, the capital of the Balkan state of Bosnia-Hertzegovina, for a public relations visit which would normally have been carried out by Emperor Franz Josef himself. Now regarding himself as getting far too old for such visits, he ordered the Heir Apparent to the Austrian throne to go as his representative. Franz Ferdinand obeyed his father as he was of the opinion that war in the Balkans could be avoided. His visit to Sarajevo had been well publicised and this gave 7 Bosnian activists the idea which would plunge the World into the first really global war.

The Archduke arrived in the Bosnian capital in the morning of 28 June and as the Royal party left to visit the office of the Mayor one of the plotters threw a small bomb at the Royal car which slid off the bonnet and exploded in the street wounding 2 police officers. The Royal party continued on its way undeterred by the incident. Whilst with the Mayor of Sarajevo the Archduke learned that the 2 officers were in hospital and he decided to change the route in order that he could visit them in hospital. This new route took the motorcade past Bosnian student and activist Gavrillo Princip and he wasted no time in carrying out his part in the ill-thought out plan. Stepping forward towards the car which had been stopped after taking a wrong turning on the new unprepared route to the hospital he fired 2 shots at the Archduke and his wife.

The Royal car sped on towards the Governors residence where the bodies of the Archduke Ferdinand and his wife Sophie were carried inside, where shortly afterwards, they were declared to be dead.

Although nothing was ever proved to indicate the involvement of any other Government, the assassination of the Heir to the Austrian throne gave Austria the excuse she needed to renew her aggression towards Serbia. From a chance spark the flame of war was to spread with lightning speed.

Although the murders at Sarajevo brought everything to a head Europe had been veering towards was at an alarming speed. Since the late 19th century Germany under Kaiser Wilhelm II had shown ambition in the rest of the world, mainly out of rivalry and jealousy of the British Empire. Germans had long believed in her superiority as a nation and longed for an Empire away from Europe. In order to protect her new colonies Germany had created a navy to rival that of Great Britain. This obvious show of strength alarmed the other nations of Europe including Britain and France.

In France the loss of Alsace and Lorraine after the Franco Prussian War of 1870 was still a source of suspicion towards anything and everything German. Germany in turn was always expecting France to try and regain those lost provinces. As Europe moved into the 20th century it was already divided into 2 armed cramps, on the one side Austria, Germany and Italy whilst on the other France, Russia and Great Britain.

The new century was barely 5 years old when Germany began to develop a war plan which would allow a campaign to be waged on 2 fronts with France and Russia. Although Chief of the German General Staff Count Von Schlieffen, after whom the plan had been named, had died in 1913 his plan remained on the table to be put into operation in August 1914.

By the summer of 1914 and after the assassination of Archduke Franz Ferdinand and his wife at Sarajevo, Austria Presented Serbia with an ultimatum which threatened its very existence as an independent state. Austria was aware that such aggression would lead to a full scale European war which if she was to be defeated would mean the end of the Austrian Empire. Emperor Franz Josef having ensured that the Kaiser was willing to give his support if required declared war on Serbia on 27 July 1914. Russia who had not been able to show ambition in Europe since her defeat by the British and

French in the Crimea in 1855 immediately aligned herself with Serbia. Although Germany had hoped to confine the conflict to a straight fight between Austria and Serbia she felt the need to send an ultimatum to Russia in an attempt to prevent her mobilizing her vast army. Russia did not reply to this threat and Germany at once declared war on Russia. This angered France as she could not stand back and leave her ally Russia to face the might of the greatest army in Europe alone.

At this stage it was not known if Great Britain would support her allies France and Russia. Britain asked both France and Germany to respect Belgium's neutrality. France readily agreed but Germany demanded a route through Belgium for her armies in order to carry out the moves planned by Count Von Schlieffen as far back as 1905. Germany declared war on neutral Belgium and Britain declared war on Germany to protect Belgium as well as her own ally France, only after Germany had again ignored the British ultimatum.

On 4 August 1914 German troops invaded Belgium and the 2 great nations of Europe were at war with each other. By 12 August the British Expeditionary Force, led by Pipers from the 2nd Battalion of the Argyll and Sutherland Highlanders, landed at Boulogne. Only 9 days later the B.E.F. was advancing to do battle with the Imperial German Army which had entered Brussels on 20 August.

As the British troops advanced in an attempt to stem the flow of the Germans they found themselves in defensive positions along the length of the Canal de Conde, through and beyond the Belgian town of Mons. The Battle of Mons which began with a dawn attack on Saturday 22 August lasted for just 2 days before the men of the British Expeditionary Force and their French allies were forced in the face of overwhelming odds to retreat. During the actions around the Mons defences the first 5 Victoria Crosses of the war were won on the first day that the British soldiers had fought as an army on European soil since the defeat of Napoleon at Waterloo on 18 June 1815.

It was during the first major action of the war that Lance Corporal Charles Jarvis from Fraserburgh, serving with the 57th Field Company of the Royal Engineers, won the first Victoria Cross to be awarded to a Scottish born soldier. At Jemappes to the west of Mons 210 Riflemen of the 1st Battalion of the Royal Scots Fusiliers were holding back almost 10 times that number of Germans. With such opposition it was inevitable that the Scots would have to withdraw across the Canal. In order to slow down the advance of the Germans it was decided that the bridge across the Canal at Jemappes would have to be destroyed. Lance Corporal Jarvis and a Private volunteered to blow up the bridge. Working for over one and a half hours in full view of the enemy and under a very heavy rifle fire the 2 soldiers finally managed to fire the charges as the oncoming German soldiers were about to cross over it. For his actions on this day the soldier from Fraserburgh was decorated with a well deserved Victoria Cross and the Private who accompanied him received an equally deserved Distinguished Conduct Medal.

By 24 August the allied armies were in full retreat in front of the German onslaught. On 26 August as they retreated the British fought the Battle of Le Cateau where they suffered nearly 8,500 casualties in a single day. Frederick Luke, a Driver serving with the 37th Battery of the Royal Field Artillery was one of 3 men from that Battery who won the Victoria Cross for attempting and succeeding to retrieve 2 Howitzers which had been abandoned to the enemy. Although not Scots born he married and lived in Glasgow after the war and become one of Scotland's best known winners of the Victoria Cross. The retreat which had begun at Mons did not end until the allied armies were at the very gates of Paris itself by the first week of September. Although the advancing German army was across the River Marne and well on course to complete Count Von Schlieffen's plan the French attacked the flank of the German First Army as it engaged the British Expeditionary Force. The attack was so concentrated that the German Commander Von Kluck felt threatened and ordered his army to turn and face the French. As a result of this the British were able to force a way into the German lines. When he realised that a serious gap had been forced in his lines Von Kluck ordered a withdrawal back across the River Marne in the direction from which they had travelled since the retreat began in the last week of August.

The forced change in the original plan to encircle Paris had cost the German High Command the advantage, which they were never really to regain throughout the remainder of the war.

Having been forced to retreat at a time when victory was within her grasp Germany decided to utilise the offensive positions on the north bank of the River Aisne. From gun positions in the heights above the river the German artillery was able to bring the allied advance to an unexpected halt. The time spent in preparing defensive works had not been wasted and they constructed a system of trenches the like of which had not been seen before.

After nearly a fortnight of bombardment, attack and counter attack neither side had gained or lost any ground and thus began what is now known in history as, "The Western Front". During these days of the Battle of the Aisne several Scottish soldiers were among those who, as a result of their gallantry, were decorated with the Victoria Cross.

The first of them was awarded to Captain William Henry Johnston, from Leith who was serving with the 59th Field Company of the Royal Engineers. As the battle raged along the banks of the river some Brigades had been able to cross the river in rafts and establish a bridgehead in the village of Saint Marguerite near Missy. This area was considered to be a death trap for the British because of its very flat nature which left them exposed to the German guns on the heights less than a mile away. Although the advanced Brigades were holding their position they were rapidly running out of ammunition. On 14 September Captain Johnston, under very heavy fire from the German artillery, worked all day in ferrying ammunition across the river to the beleaguered Brigades and on the return journey taking aback wounded men. By his actions the men of the 14th and 15th Brigades were able to consolidate their bridgehead across the river beneath the German guns.

Less than 10 miles away on the same day Edinburgh born Private George Wilson of the 2nd Battalion of The Highland Light Infantry won the second Victoria Cross of this battle. The 5th Brigade of which the Highland Light Infantry was part of were being held up in their advance by accurate and deadly fire from a well protected German machine gun near the village of Verneuil. Volunteering to attack the position Private Wilson accompanied by another Private of his Regiment set out, the 2 men had not gone far when his companion was killed. Continuing alone Private Wilson eventually reached the gun and immediately shot the officer in charge and entered the emplacement and continued to shoot or bayonet the rest of the crew. Having completed his task he calmly walked back to his own lines with the captured gun.

The third Scottish born winner on that day was Hurlford in Ayrshire born Private Ross Tollerton of the 1st Battalion of the Queen's Own Cameron Highlanders. On this day the men of the Camerons were experiencing their first taste of the type of fighting which was to typify the Great War and in this their first engagement suffered many casualties. Having been forced to attack well prepared German positions this left many men wounded and lying in exposed situations. Private Tollerton on seeing Lieutenant Matheson of his own Regiment lying in a very exposed place went forward and removed him to a place of relative safety. Later when the Battalion was forced to withdraw Private Tollerton returned to his officer and remained with him behind the enemy lines. Although twice wounded himself the 2 men stayed hidden for 3 days and even although the Cameron Private was 6 foot 2 inches tall they were not detected. When he felt able to do so he was able to lead to the safety of the British lines Lieutenant Matheson. For his bravery and devotion to his officer during the time he was behind the enemy lines Private Tollerton was decorated with the Victoria Cross.

The last of the Scots to be awarded the Victoria Cross during the Battle of the Aisne was Captain Harry Ranken of the Royal Army Medical Corps. At the time of the action which was to result in the award of the Country's highest decoration for bravery Glasgow born Captain Ranken was attached to the 1st Battalion of the King's Royal Rifle Corps. On the evening of 19 September the enemy began to show increased activity. Throughout the day the number of attacks on positions around Haute-Avesnes increased. Each time the enemy was repulsed with great losses. During one of these attacks Captain Ranken was severely wounded in the leg as he went about his battlefield duties. He took a little time to stem the flow of blood from his own wound before continuing to attend to the wounded. Although asked on several occasions to go to the rear to have his own wound attended to he steadfastly refused. As time went by he was conscious that his own wound would need to be attended to and it was the next day before he allowed himself to be taken to the rear for medical treatment. Alas it was too late and he died a short while later. For his dedication to his duty towards the other wounded men on the battlefield Captain Ranken was awarded the first posthumous Victoria Cross to a Scottish born soldier of the Great War.

After the Battle of the Aisne both the Germans and the Allies were determined not to allow themselves to be outflanked by the other. After the indecision of the battle and the formation of static defences the length of the front moved towards the sea and the occupation of the channel ports. By the leap frogging action the front soon extended from the sea in the north to almost the Italian border in the South.

The month of October 1914 saw the start of what was to become known as the First Battle of Ypres. In 1914 this battle was to be the final attempt by the German Army to break through the Allied line of defence in the West and once through, the Channel Ports would be at their mercy. The general concept of the First Battle of Ypres was one of small scale battles fought over the many little towns all along the length of the front. It was during one of these many actions around the town of La Bassee that the first Victoria Cross of the war was won by a soldier serving in the Cameronians (Scottish Rifles). It was awarded to Private Henry May (fig.7) from Glasgow, who was serving in the 1st Battalion, for rescuing wounded comrades. On 22 October at La Boutillerie in the northern sector of the battle area Private May went out into No Man's Land to rescue a soldier who was lying wounded in an exposed position. Unfortunately before the Glasgow soldier could reach him the man was shot and killed. Later on in the same day he again went out alone to open ground in front of the enemy's guns and rescued an officer who was lying seriously wounded. When he reached the officer Private May carried him across his shoulders and dashed over 300 yards back across the machine gun swept area to safety.

On Thursday 29 October when there was a break in the atrocious weather which had been a feature of the early stages of the battle the Germans launched a determined counter attack. During this attack which was centred near Gheluvelt on the Ypres to Menin road the men of the 2nd Battalion of The Gordon Highlanders were conspicuous in their gallantry when they were able to regain trenches which had been lost to the Germans in the initial onslaught. These counter attacks on the lost trenches were led by Newhills in Aberdeenshire born Lieutenant James Brooke. Moving under heavy rifle and machine gun fire Lieutenant Brooke led his men with great coolness and speed which resulted in the recapture of the trenches at a time when a general counter offensive could not have been organised. When he had secured the lost trenches he himself decided to go to the rear to bring back support to consolidate the gained ground. Unfortunately whilst making his way back to the rear this gallant officer was shot and killed. For his skill in regaining the lost trenches against overwhelming odds Lieutenant Brooke was awarded a posthumous Victoria Cross. Although at the time of his death he held the rank of Lieutenant he had in fact been promoted to Captain although that did not appear in the London Gazette until after his death.

On 11 November 1914 the last day of the First Battle of Ypres near Becelaere, to the north of Gheluvelt, Edinburgh born Captain Walter Brodie of the 2nd Battalion of the Highland Light Infantry led a charge to remove German troops from a section of British trench which had previously been lost to them. The British counter attacks had caused the enemy to abandon most of their gains of the battle. However there were still a few of the enemy who were stubbornly holding onto their gains. During the attack to remove the enemy from the captured trenches Captain Brodie personally bayoneted several of the defenders and by his actions a potentially dangerous situation was averted. As a result of the action of Captain Brodie and his men over 80 of the enemy were killed and a further 51 were taken prisoner. For leading his men on such a dangerous attack Captain Brodie was decorated with the second Victoria Cross of the war to be won by a soldier serving in the 2nd Battalion of The Highland Light Infantry.

As the war on the land raged in the trenches of the Western Front, the war in East Africa was being waged with a lot less publicity and glamour. It was felt by the British Generals that the war in the German Colonies would be quickly brought to a conclusion. British and German troops were facing each other across the borders of British and German East Africa. Apart from the problems of climate the British Commander in East Africa had to make do without sufficient resources of a quality to conduct a full scale campaign against the enemy. At the start of the war in Europe the Colonial Army was totally unprepared. As troops were urgently needed to fight in the Western Front against the Germans, only half trained and even less acclimatised troops were sent to support local Regiments in Africa. In the east of Africa the Imperial German Navy seemed able to come and go as it pleased to attack British shipping without fear of attack. These attacks prompted the Royal Navy to increase its presence in the area. After several setbacks in the battles to secure land supremacy the Royal Navy remained in sufficient strength. The old battleship H.M.S. Goliath on 28 November sailed into the enemy held port of Dar-es-salaam to search the port and carry out necessary demolitions. The Second in Command of the old battleship was Edinburgh born Commander Henry Ritchie (fig.8) whose task was to see that the demolitions were carried out. In order to carry out this work Commander Ritchie had fitted out one of Goliath's steam pinnaces. The pinnace along with 2 other small craft entered the harbour and caught the enemy unawares by the approach in the small craft. Commander Ritchie and his men were well inside the harbour before they were spotted. In spite of the attention from the enemy shore guns the 3 small craft continued with their tasks of searching and demolition. During this work the Edinburgh sailor was wounded 8 times in the space of only 20 minutes. Refusing to be treated he continued to direct operations until he fainted from loss of blood. Commander Ritchie recovered from his wounds to receive the first Naval Victoria Cross of the war as well as the first ever to be awarded to a Scottish born sailor.

Meanwhile back at the Western Front the pace of the war had slowed down to the extent that it was now almost static. Any small gain by either side was almost immediately cancelled out by a counter attack which would probably gain literally a few yards for the counter attackers. It was during one of these many counter attacks that Lieutenant William Bruce, who was born in Edinburgh, won the next Victoria Cross awarded to a Scotsman. On 19 December near Givenchy in the sector north of Arras, Lieutenant Bruce an officer in the 59 Scinde Rifles (Indian Army) led a small group of his soldiers and captured an enemy held trench. Although suffering from a wound in his neck he calmly walked up and down the captured trench encouraging his men to stand fast against the several counter attacks which had taken place. Despite the shower of bombs raining down on them and the concentrated rifle fire the Indians held their ground all day. As dusk fell the enemy attacked once more in strength and finally overran the trench and captured the remnants of Lieutenant Bruce's Regiment. In the final moments of the struggle the gallant Scot lost his life. Although the action in which Lieutenant Bruce won his Victoria Cross took place in December 1914 and made his the tenth award to a Scot it was not until 4 September 1919 that his award appeared in the London Gazette.

On the same day as Lieutenant Bruce died winning his Victoria Cross at a place called Rouges Bancs near Neuve Chapelle a young Private in the 2nd Battalion of the Scots Guards rescued a severely wounded man from under the very noses of the Germans. A soldier was lying in a very exposed position in front of the enemy trenches and had been the subject of an unsuccessful rescue attempt by a stretcher party. When the rescue was abandoned Private James MacKenzie from New Abbey in Kirkcudbright went out under a very heavy fire and brought the wounded man back to safety. Later in the same day the gallant Guardsman was killed trying to rescue another wounded men in a similar situation. For his actions on this day at Rouges Bancs the young Scot was decorated with a posthumous Victoria Cross.

As the war in the Western Front moved into the next year of war the remainder of 1914 was remarkable only for the unofficial Christmas truce of which much has been written.

The early part of 1915 continued much as 1914 had ended with little action on the Western Front although things were beginning to hot up in the African and Asian Fronts.

The beginning of February had seen increased fighting in and around the town of Cuinchy. Although there were no major battles with the Germans in France the war with them in Eastern Africa continued to give concern when the town of Jassin surrendered to the Germans. The nationalist rebels in South Africa were taking advantage of the difficult situation the British found themselves in. In an expression of German sympathy the Boers revolted after the British invaded German South West Africa. Further north the Turks had moved into and occupied the town of Katiyeh which was so close to the Suez Canal that it posed a threat to the British supply lines from the Empire. From Katiyeh the Turks launched their first attack on the Suez Canal in late January 1915.

In his sixth despatch of the war Field Marshal Sir John French reported that at the end of February 2, "many vital considerations induced me to believe that a vigorous offensive movement by the forces under my command should be planned and carried out at the earliest possible moment".

These offensive operations resulted in a 15 minute bombardment of the village of Neuve Chapelle on the morning of 10 March 1915 followed by the advance of 14 Battalions against the German defences in the area. This independent operation by the British was a very expensive gamble to keep up the morale of the British soldiers who were beginning to suffer as a result of long periods of inactivity. Although this battle lasted for 3 days all the major gains were won in the first 3 hours of the attack. After the initial successes the second line of German defences were encountered and for the remainder of the battle many thousands of men on both sides were sacrificed.

It was on the second day of the Battle of Neuve Chapelle that Elgin born Corporal William Anderson serving in the 2nd Battalion of the Yorkshire Regiment won the first Victoria Cross of 1915 to be awarded to a Scottish born soldier. Advancing through Neuve Chapelle Corporal Anderson led 3 men of his own Regiment to remove a party of Germans who had taken a section of the British trenches. Armed with bombs the Corporal and his 3 men attacked the enemy. After he had thrown all of his own bombs he continued to throw the bombs of his comrades who had all been wounded by this point in the skirmish. When all the bombs had been thrown he continued alone along the trench system firing his rifle. The position was secured and the brave Scot died of his wound the next day and was later decorated with a posthumous Victoria Cross for his prompt and determined action which saved what could have become a very serious situation.

From the outbreak of hostilities in August 1914 Britain and her Allies had been fighting mainly in France and Flanders in what was for the most part a defensive campaign. However the conflict had moved to other fronts in other parts of the world. The war in East and West Africa had been fairly localised affairs which were being handled by mainly Empire troops who had been hastily sent by Lord Kitchener in preference to the apparently better trained troops who were fighting in the Western Front. The need to open up another front on a similar scale to that being fought over the towns and villages of France and Belgium and return to the Allies to the offensive was discussed in the War Cabinet from the very earliest days of January 1915.

The internal warring of the Admirals and Generals as to the best way of capturing Constantinople and forcing Turkey out of the war enabled leaks to appear in the veil of secrecy which should have surrounded such planning. So much so that when it was agreed that the plan formulated by the very inexperienced Admiral Carden to put into action for a Naval Force to make its way through the Dardanelles the enemy seemed to be well prepared. When this move resulted in failure after nearly a month of attempts by the Navy to break the Turkish defences inside the forts which guarded the entrance to the Dardanelles all the element of surprise was lost as to the Allies intentions for the area.

The failure of this operation coupled with the French announcement that she already had troops stationed in Egypt ready to occupy the Gallipoli peninsula alerted the world and the Turks as to what could be expected very shortly.

On Sunday morning 25 April 1915 the British Expeditionary Force and troops from the Dominions, who had been gathering and training for many weeks in the sun and sand of Egypt moved slowly towards the shores which had been chosen for the landings. At 4.50am a Turkish searchlight started to sweep the sea close to the shore and suddenly the whole coastline was swept by murderous rifle and machine gun fire as the invaders tried to gain that first foothold in Gallipoli. In order to capture as swiftly as possible the 50 mile long peninsula landings were made at several places all along the coast. The Australians landed on a beach north of Gaba Tepe, the Royal Fusiliers and part of the Naval Division also landed in the same area and to the west of Cape Helles the Lancashire Fusiliers landed and performed with such outstanding gallantry that men of the 1st Battalion won 6 Victoria Crosses before breakfast on the morning of the landings. To the east of Cape Helles a converted Steamer the "River Clyde" beached herself as far inshore as possible and disgorged 2,000 troops whose task on landing was to thrust inland and attack to the rear of the defenders of Cape Helles.

It was during the efforts to land these troops that the next Victoria Crosses were won by 5 sailors on board the "River Clyde". They were Acting Captain Edward Unwin, Midshipman George Drewry, Midshipman Wilfred Malleson, Able Seaman William Williams and Carnoustie born Seaman George Samson. The Scot was one of the 4 sailors who helped Captain Unwin get the lighters from the ship to the shore. The Seaman of the Royal Naval Reserve worked on a lighter a small flat bottomed boat used for unloading vessels anchored at a distance from the wharf all day under very heavy and accurate fire attending to the wounded and getting lines out. During the day he carried out many daring rescues of wounded men until he himself was severely wounded by machine gun fire. When he was eventually treated he was found to have 19 wounds on his body. However he recovered to receive at Buckingham Palace on 5 October the first Victoria Cross to be awarded to a Royal Naval Reserve Rating and the second to a Scottish sailor.

Although the fighting in Gallipoli continued for many more months the next 3 awards to Scotsmen of the Country's highest decoration for bravery were made to soldiers serving in the trenches of the Western Front.

In early May of 1915 the front had moved very little from that which had been defended with so much cost at the Battle of Neuve Chapelle in March. At Aubers Ridge in the same part of the front the British Commanders had not yet discovered how best to deal with the German trench system. The effectiveness of the German machine gun in strongly defended trenches was still causing unacceptable numbers of casualties amongst the British soldiers sent out to attack such fortifications. On 9 May Corporal John Ripley a soldier in the 1st Battalion of the Black Watch led his section of the platoon against the enemy trenches at Rue de Bois to the south of Neuve Chapelle and was the first man to climb into the enemy position. From this vantage point he directed his men towards Gaps in the German wire entanglements. Then taking his own section through a break in the second line of German defences he established a defensive post and held it until all his men had been killed or wounded. Corporal Ripely who was born in Keith recovered from a severe head wound to receive a well deserved Victoria Cross for his determination on this occasion when he broke through 3 lines of German defences.

On the same day another soldier from the Black Watch, this time the 2nd Battalion, was also awarded the Victoria Cross for gallantry at Rue de Bois. He was Lance Corporal David Finlay from Guardbridge in Fife. Whilst leading a party of bombers in the attack on that day 10 of his men were killed or wounded, undeterred he and 2 of the survivors continued with the bombing mission. On the way forward the Lance Corporal was knocked unconscious for about 10 minutes. On regaining his senses he noticed that one of the 2 survivors was lying wounded in an exposed situation in front of the enemy's guns. He reached this man and without consideration for his own safety he dressed the man's wounds before he dragged him back to the safety of the British lines.

In was on 12 June that the next Scottish Victoria Cross was won. A party of men from the Lanarkshire Territorial Battalion (8th) of the Highland Light Infantry had gone out into No Man's Land in order to destroy an enemy barricade. The party was led by a popular young officer by the name of Lieutenant Martin. In the heat of the fighting near the barricade a mine was exploded and the Territorials returned to their own lines. On return it was found that Lieutenant Martin was missing. Although some of the men had gone out in the dark to try and locate him it was impossible to find him. However at daybreak he was seen moving about obviously wounded, a few feet from the parapet of a German trench, whose occupants were making efforts to try and kill him. Permission was given for only one man to try and rescue the Lieutenant as it was pointed out to the many volunteers that the attempt would probably mean certain death. Although he was born in Armadale in West Lothian Lance Corporal William Angus was chosen because he lived in Carluke the same village as Lieutenant Martin. The Lance Corporal who before the war had played for Glasgow Celtic Football Club dashed out into the open and because of his level of fitness was able to reach the officer without being wounded. The Germans were soon aware of the rescue attempt and started to lob bombs over the parapet. These bombs when they went off sent up a cloud of dust which was used to good advantage by Lance Corporal Angus as he made his way back to his own trenches. Lance Corporal Angus who had received about 40 wounds on his way back from the rescue recovered to be presented with the Victoria Cross by King George V at Buckingham Palace later in the year.

As the war continued in the fields and villages of France and Belgium the invasion which had taken place in the Gallipoli peninsula had also failed to bring about the desired effect, i.e. the removal of Turkey from the war, with the result that the British and Colonial troops involved had to settle into a trench style warfare similar to that being experienced on the Western Front. Faced with an enemy fighting on its own soil the Allied Commanders had underestimated the courage of the Turks. The effort put in by both sides to win relatively insignificant objectives resulted in the war of attrition grinding to a halt as both adversaries became totally exhausted. By the end of July the campaign had stopped and the heat of the summer with its disease ridden flies began to take more of a toll than the bullets of the enemy.

On 13 August men of the 1/4th Battalion of the Royal Scots Fusiliers were engaged in retaking a trench which had previously been lost to the Turks when Private David Ross Lauder (fig.36), a Carter from Dalry before he joined the Royal Scots Fusiliers, threw a bomb which unfortunately failed to clear the parapet of the trench and instead of landing amongst the Turks fell into the midst of the Fusiliers. Immediately realising the danger to his comrades Private Lauder shouted a warning and put his foot on the smoking bomb. As he did this the bomb exploded and because his foot was covering the device the effect was minimised. By his prompt and unselfish action to redeem his own mistake Private Lauder saved the lives of 7 men, a sergeant and an officer. His right foot was so mutilated that it had to be amputated before he could be removed to hospital in Malta. Whilst he was recovering from his wound in Malta he heard that he had been awarded the Country's highest decoration for bravery and at the same time he heard that the Serbian government were so impressed by his self sacrifice that he was also awarded Serbia's Medal for Bravery.

During the early part of 1915 it was already evident to both the British and French High Commands that the level of co-operation was about as low as it could get. This prompted the 2 Governments to develop a strategic plan to speed up the defeat of Germany. It was agreed that a joint attack would take place in that part of the line around the town of Loos on 25 September 1915. The French artillery had been bombarding the German lines for 3 weeks and when on the morning of 25 September the guns stopped the Germans knew what to expect, as what happened next was now almost tradition. The Germans returned to the trenches from their almost bomb proof dugouts and awaited the infantry attack. On this occasion the French restarted the bombardment and caused many casualties in the German lines.

To the north of the town the British had attacked the German trenches on the cessation of the artillery bombardment. Waiting for a breeze to blow towards the enemy the order was given for the release of 150 tons of chlorine gas. The light breeze which was to carry the gas towards the Germans changed direction and wafted the gas back to the British lines. It was during this attack that the Great War's most famous Scots Victoria Cross was won by a Piper from Little Swinton in Berwickshire who was serving in the 7th Battalion of The King's Own Scottish Borders. When he noticed that his Company was shaken by the effects of gas Piper Daniel Laidlaw, with a complete disregard for his own safety stood up on the parapet of the trench and marching backwards and forwards played Regimental Marches to encourage his men. The effect of this was to rally the men who went forward and won their objective. The Berwickshire Piper continued to play in spite of having been wounded and only stopped when the enemy had been routed.

As the battle moved into a second day the men of the 15th (Scottish) Division had advanced through Loos and were pressing on Hill 70. It was on the attack to capture this vantage point in the battle that Private Robert Dunsire (fig.10) from Buckhaven in Fife rescued a wounded man from No Man's Land. Later in the day a cry for help was heard from a position a lot closer to the German lines. Again the brave Scot who was serving in the 13th Battalion of the Royal Scots went out and with complete disregard for his own safety found the man and carried him back into the British trenches. For his actions on this day Private Robert Dunsire was awarded a well deserved Victoria Cross but unfortunately he did not live long enough to have it bestowed upon him as he was killed in action at Mazingarbe on 30 January 1916.

As the battles which collectively became known as the Battle of Loos continued the next 2 awards of the Victoria Cross have a lot in common. They were both won in or near a prominent feature known as Hohenzollern Redoubt, both recipients came from Clackmannanshire and they were cousins.

The first of them was awarded to Corporal James Pollock of the 5th (Service) Battalion of the Queen's Own Cameron Highlanders. On 25 September the 5th Camerons had been given orders to capture a trench known as "Little Willie". Although the Highlanders were in control of a redoubt on 27 September the Germans in great numbers were beginning to regain the captured trench and threaten the redoubt which the Camerons were defending. After having been given permission Corporal Pollock left the relative safety of the redoubt and crossed the open ground which enabled him to outflank the enemy bombers who were moving along the trench. When he was within throwing distance of the enemy he stood on top of the parapet below which they were passing and attacked them with his own bombs. In spite of being wounded twice he was able to force them back along "Little Willie" and thus prevented the Hohenzellern Redoubt from falling into the hands of the enemy. For his action in securing the redoubt the Tillicoultry born soldier was decorated with the first Victoria Cross in his family.

The second award to the family from Tillicoultry was won by the cousin of Corporal Pollock, Corporal James Dawson. It was on 13 October again at the Hohenzollern Redoubt that Corporal Dawson, who was serving in the 187th Company of the Royal Engineers, performed with outstanding gallantry during a gas attack. The trenches were full of men waiting to go forward when the system began to fill with gas. Corporal Dawson in full view of the enemy walked up and down the section of the trench giving clear instructions to his Sappers to remove men from those parts full of the gas. He later found 3 gas containers which were leaking gas and rolled them closer to the enemy trenches. Throughout this time he was being fired upon by the enemy. He then returned to cover where he fired shots into the containers in order to disperse the gas more quickly. His coolness and gallantry on this occasion undoubtedly saved many lives and the gallant Corporal was decorated with the Victoria Cross.

The last Scottish born winner of the Victoria Cross in 1915 was Glasgow born Private William Young who was serving in the 8th (Service) Battalion of the East Lancashire Regiment. On 22 December east of Fonquvillers in France Private Young saw from his position that Sergeant Allan from his own Regiment was lying in front of the German wire. On his own initiative the Maryhill man climbed out of his trench and crawled to the wounded man. Sergeant Allan called to him and told him to go back into cover. Having ignored this command from the Non Commissioned Officer he continued and was wounded in the chest and jaw. Even this did not stop the gallant Scot and with the assistance of another man he was able to bring the Sergeant back and thus saved his life. When Private Young eventually got the wounded man back to safety he walked alone back to a dressing station to have his own wounds attended to. However the brave Scot did not live long enough to actually wear his medal as he died in hospital at Aldershot whilst undergoing a relatively simple operation on his wounded jaw on 28 August 1916.

When the war moved into yet another year the Commanders were again looking at ways of ending it before the end of 1916. On 5 January there was a bill before Parliament to give Britain that most needed of commodities, conscripted men.

In February of this year the French became involved in the German assault on the fortifications around the town of Verdun. The battle for Verdun soon became a centre into which all of France's reserves were concentrated. As the rest of the world waited to see the outcome of this power struggle the war in the west came to a virtual standstill and this meant that the British Armies had control of the whole front from Ypres to the Somme.

In the middle of May the fighting around Vimy Ridge eased as if to signal the build up of a great offensive. The great offensive which was expected did not take place on land but on 31 May 1916 began the only great Naval battle of the whole war, the Battle of Jutland.

In the Western Front the use of mines with their vast tunnelling works had increased with both sides now committed to using this tactic. In the middle of June the Germans increased their pressure on the French defenders at Verdun and the British in an effort to relieve some of that pressure kept up the attacks from the section of the front controlled by them. On 22 June at Givenchy in the north men of the 5th Battalion of the Cameronians (Scottish Rifles) were consolidating their position in the crater caused by the explosion of an enormous mine. Sergeant John Erskine from Dunfermline on seeing a sergeant and a private soldier from his own Regiment lying wounded in No Man's Land rushed out under a continuous fire and was able to bring both men back to the safety of the crater. Later in the same day when he noticed a movement from what he had thought was the body of one of his officers the brave Sergeant again went out to the aid of the wounded man. On reaching the officer he bandaged his head wound and remained with him for fully an hour. When assistance eventually arrived by his men digging a shallow trench out to where the two men lay, Sergeant Erskine shielded the officer with his own body to prevent him being wounded or even killed by the attentive rifle fire. For his actions throughout the day the gallant Sergeant Erskine was decorated with the Victoria Cross. At Arras in April 1917 Sergeant Erskine was killed in action and became yet another of Scotland's Victoria Cross winners who did not live enough to enjoy his new found fame.

As all previous offenses in the Western Front had been preceded by a continuous barrage for several days or even weeks at 7.30am on the first day of July 1916 the guns fell silent. The German defenders all along the front knew what to expect as did those thousands of men who had to walk across No Man's Land. They had thought that the firing of many thousands of tons of high explosive shells into the German wire entanglements and trenches would have destroyed everything.

As wave after wave of Britain's young men walked towards the enemy lines confident that the barrage had done its job, a whole generation of them would not be alive to record how they felt on that first day of the Battle of The Somme as they walked calmly to their death. On this day of infamy a total of 9 Victoria Crosses were won to reflect in a small way the courage of these thousands of men who fought and died on that day. Of the 9 won on that day 2 were awarded to Scottish born soldiers serving in 2 of Scotland's most famous Regiments.

The first of these was won by Walter Ritchie, who had joined the army as a Drummer while still under age. Having transferred into the 2nd Battalion of the Seaforth Highlanders he had seen action with them since the start of hostilities in 1914. On 1 July whilst the Highlanders were attacking north of Beaumont Hamel Drummer Ritchie without being ordered to do so stood on top of the parapet of the trench which had just been captured and repeatedly sounded the charge to rally the men of his and other Regiments who having lost most of their officers and non commissioned officers were wavering and beginning to retire. Throughout the action the Glasgow born Drummer showed courage and initiative of the highest order.

The second Victoria Cross of the day to be awarded to a Scot was won by Sergeant James Turnbull of Glasgow serving in the 17th (Glasgow Commercials) Battalion of the Highland Light Infantry. On that day at Authuille on the Somme front Sergeant Turnbull was one of a party of the Light Infantry who had captured the Liepzig Salient which was of some importance to the enemy. They immediately began a series of counter attacks to try and dislodge the Glasgow men. Very soon the holding group had to be replenished with reinforcements as the defenders were killed or wounded but Sergeant Turnbull never gave up his determination to defend the position to the last. At times almost single handed he beat off repeated attacks of his hard won position by an equally determined enemy. Throughout the whole encounter Sergeant Turnbull displayed the highest degree of skill in the performance of his duties. As the day was ending he was shot and killed by a sniper as he defended the Liepzig Salient against further attacks by the enemy bombers.

While the Battles of the Somme continued, in East Africa another Scots born soldier was winning yet another Victoria Cross for Scotland. On 24 August 1916 at a place called Mlali Captain William Bloomfield serving in the Scout Corps of the 2nd South African Mounted Brigade was leading the pursuit of the Germans when they decided to counter attack. The Edinburgh born officer who had emigrated to South Africa noticed a Corporal who was wounded and had been left behind as the South Africans had been forced to withdraw. At considerate risk to himself Captain Bloomfield went out and carried the wounded Corporal over 400 yards of machine gun swept ground to safety. For this act showing the highest degree of valour and endurance the Scots born South African was decorated with a well deserved Victoria Cross.

As the Battle of the Somme continued along its indecisive course the next Scottish born winner of the Country's highest decoration for bravery Piper John Richardson was serving in the 16th Battalion of the Manitoba Regiment (Canadian Scottish). On 8 October at Regina Trench near Thiepval the Canadians were being held up by strong wire defences and rifle fire. Bellshill born Piper Richardson had been given permission to play his pipes as the men went over the top so he stood on top of the parapet playing Regimental tunes. His playing inspired the men to rush the enemy and capture the position. Later the Piper was ordered to help escort prisoners to the rear and had only gone a short distance when he realised that he had left his beloved pipes behind and insisted in returning to collect them. Piper Richardson was never seen again. The gallant Piper was the first of several Scots serving in the Canadian Expeditionary Forces to receive the Empire's highest decoration for distinguished conduct.

The last Victoria Cross of 1916 to be won by a Scot was that awarded to Glasgow born Robert Downie. On 23 October east of Lesboeufs at a time when most of the officers of his Regiment, the 2nd Battalion of the Royal Dublin Fusiliers, had become casualties Sergeant Downie in complete disregard for his own safety moved about under heavy fire and organised an attack which had temporarily faltered. At a critical moment he rushed forward shouting "Come on the Dubs" at which point the line joined him in the attack. The Glasgow soldier personally accounted for several of the enemy and captured a machine gun and its crew. Although he had been wounded early on in the attack he remained with his men giving valuable assistance while the captured position was being consolidated. As a result of his determination on this day Sergeant Downie was decorated with the Victoria Cross to go along side the Military Medal and the 2 Mentions in Despatches he already had been awarded.

As the war was not to be won by the end of 1916 there was yet another year of war in which more Scots would win further Victoria Crosses.

By the end of 1916 neither side was any nearer to winning the war and as it continued into yet another year there was renewed efforts to bring the conflict to a speedy conclusion.

Although there had been peace initiatives during the previous year the truth was that the Allies did not wish the war to end with such indecision.

The year had begun with further German attacks on Verdun and increased activity on the British sector of the front. The French had envisaged the final victory coming from a major offensive in their sector coupled with diversionary attacks from the length of the British trenches. The Germans as if sensing such a move by the Allies used the early part of 1917 to withdraw and shorten the line of defence by moving to a previously prepared position known as the Hindenburg Line. During this early part of 1917 the British had success at Beamount Hamel, the scene of the gallant work done by the Highlanders of the 51st (Highland) Division in the fighting in the first phase of the Battle of the Somme in July 1916. This was followed in late February on the River Ancre by further successes.

On the 10 March 1917 in the Atlantic Ocean about 350 miles east of the Azores a New Zealand Shipping Company ship named the "Otaki", converted into an armed merchantman with a 4.7 inch gun mounted for defensive purposes only, encountered the German surface raider the "Moewe". The armament of the German ship consisted of four 5.9 inch, one 4.1 inch and two 22 pounder guns as well as torpedo tubes. The enemy Captain observed the "Otaki" for some time before ordering her to stop. When the Master of the "Otaki" Archibald Bisset Smith heard this order he immediately opened fire on the German ship. The duel between the 2 ships lasted about 20 minutes, during which the Gunner on the "Otaki" scored hits on the enemy 7 times and caused a fire which burned for 3 days. When the Merchant Master realised that his ship had sustained severe damage he ordered that the ships lifeboats were lowered to allow his crew to escape and be rescued by the German ship. Archibald Smith, who was born in Cults in Aberdeenshire, remained with his ship as she went to the bottom of the ocean with the Red Ensign still flying. For his courage in tackling a larger and better armed vessel and remaining with his ship in the finest of naval tradition the gallant Merchant Navy Officer was awarded a posthumous Victoria Cross. When the announcement of his decoration appeared in the London Gazette he was given an honorary Royal Naval Reserve rank to allow him to receive the award.

As the year passed the successes of the British and Empire Forces mounted and the whole line moved nearer the Hindenburg Line. A day late on 9 April the offensive began which was to result in the breakthrough at Arras and ended with the Canadian Infantry on Vimy Ridge after some of the most bitter fighting of the war to that point. The capture of Vimy is still remembered in Canada to this day by a group of people who after more than three quarters of a century still recognise the gallantry of these brave Canadians. The true value of this piece of France was only realised when the casualty list was published, 11,000 Canadians killed, wounded or missing in less than a week of fighting. Amongst those killed was Wishaw born Private William Milne serving in the 16th Battalion of the Manitoba Regiment (Canadian Scottish). Private Milne was in the area near Thelus on the approach to the first objective of his Battalion in an area known as Zwolfe Graben. As his section moved towards this objective the Scot noticed a German machine gun firing and causing many casualties amongst the Canadians. Crawling forward on his hands and knees he succeeded in killing the crew and capturing the gun. After this capture Private Milne re turned to the firing line where almost immediately another gun was discovered. Again as before he stalked the gun and this time was able to capture the crew as well as the gun. Shortly after the second gun was cleared the gallant soldier was killed as he advanced towards the final capture of the Ridge. For his gallantry on this day the Canadian from Wishaw was decorated with a posthumous Victoria Cross the second such award to a Scot serving with the Canadian Scottish.

After the Canadians had behaved so gallantly at Vimy Ridge the advance from Arras continued towards the north of Fampoux where the 2nd Battalion of the Seaforth Highlanders had penetrated the German defences to a depth of over 4 miles. After such a gain the Battalion became engaged in the bitter close quarter trench warfare, which had been a feature of the fighting in the area for many months. On 11 April when the Battalion was ordered to attack a Chemical Works at Roeux Lieutenant Donald Mackintosh, who was born in Glasgow, was shot in the leg during the advance. In spite of being crippled he led his men until they had captured an enemy trench. Once in possession of the trench he and his men had to repel several counter attacks by the enemy as they tried to regain the lost trench. Although he was wounded again he steadfastly refused to relinquish command of his men. By this time he was unable to stand yet he still organised the remaining 15 men under his command to attack the final objective at which point he was again wounded, this time fatally. For his outstanding gallantry Lieutenant Mackintosh was decorated with a well deserved Victoria Cross, unfortunately posthumously. King George V presented his medal to the brave Lieutenant's mother and father at a ceremony in Buckingham Palace later that year.

In spite of the offensive in Gallipoli and the continued fighting around the River Tigris in Mesopotamia the Turks were showing little sign of weakening. The winter rains in the area had turned the desert into a sea of mud which made effective campaigning impossible. After the fall of Baghdad on 13 March the British forces moved out into the desert in order to capitalise on recent successes and met with a Turkish defence force at the town called Istabulat on the banks of the River Tigris. It was here, on 21 April 1917, that Private Charles Melvin (fig.9) from Kirriemuir, serving with the 2nd Battalion of the Black Watch, was waiting for reinforcements before venturing to attack a Turkish front line trench system. Lying within 50 yards of the enemy in ground swept by rifle and machine gun fire Private Melvin, without hesitation, leapt from his place of safety in his trench and dashed across the open ground. On reaching the enemy position he stood above the trench and fired 2 shots at the enemy. When the Turks realised what was happening they replied and fired back at the brave Scot and he immediately jumped on top of them with his bayonet in his hand. After he had killed 2 of the enemy the others in the trench fled from the bayonet wielding Scot, leaving several dead and one wounded man behind. Having gathered up some prisoners he marched them across the very same ground over which he had charged and delivered them to a waiting officer. Once he had completed his one man charge he returned to his position in the line and waited for the reinforcements. For his dash and daring Private Melvin was awarded a well deserved Victoria Cross.

Meanwhile on the same day back in the Arras front the Allies were still trying to breakthrough. In the trench fighting in and around the village of Fontaine-les-Croiselles men of the 2nd Battalion of the Argyll and Sutherland Highlanders distinguished themselves. Amongst the officers of this Battalion was Acting Captain Arthur Henderson who behaved with outstanding gallantry as he led men of his company against enemy held trenches. As the Argyll's moved out to attack the enemy Captain Henderson was almost immediately wounded in the left arm. Oblivious to this wound he stayed with his men and was at their head when the enemy front line trench was captured. As their front line had been penetrated the Germans massed their troops in an effort to regain this lost ground. The wounded Captain at once realised the danger from enemy machine gunners and bombers and set about consolidating the hard won position. The workrate of this Officer in preparing his men for the inevitable onslaught by an enemy who outnumbered his company of Highlanders by about 10 to 1, was not diminished by the severity of the wound he had received. This gallant officer went abut his duties to his men with the vigour of a man in full fitness and totally unconcerned by the fact that the enemy were firing on his position from a very short range, so much so that each German assault was met with the most stubborn resistance. As reinforcements were making their way forward to the beleaguered Argyll's, the enemy in frustration as much as anything launched what was to be their final attempt to regain their lost trench. When this was eventually beaten off Captain Henderson continued to move amongst his men reassuring them until help could arrive instead of having his wounds attended to. Almost at the very moment when help arrived this brave officer was again wounded, this time fatally, and he fell into the bottom of the trench which he had done so much to defend where he died. Unable to carry his body to the rear the Highlanders with heavy hearts of the trench this officer, who had already been decorated with the Military Cross for his courage during the early days of the Battle of the Somme in July 1916, was awarded a well deserved but posthumous Victoria Cross. Both Captain Henderson's decorations were presented to his father by His Majesty King George at a special ceremony at Buckingham Palace on 21 July 1917.

Throughout the remainder of April and into May 1917 the battles around the town of Arras raged. On 3 May the Canadians who had behaved so gallantly at the capture of Vimy Ridge now pushed the front line to the outskirts of the town of Acheville, where Lieutenant Robert Combe, who was born in Aberdeen, with the remnants of his men from the 27th Battalion of the Manitoba Regiment had come under an intense bombardment from the enemy. When the Canadians reached their objective Lieutenant Combe had only 5 men left with him after a runner had been sent to the rear to summon help. With his 5 men the brave Lieutenant continued with the advantage gained to attack the enemy with bombs instead of consolidating the position. In doing this he inflicted many casualties on the enemy. In the course of his advance through the enemy trench system the small band had gathered up more than 80 prisoners. When the runner returned with help they found the trench littered with dead and dying Germans and also the of body of Lieutenant Combe who had been shot in the head by a sniper at the very moment of his triumph. For his outstanding leadership, when he was at the head of his men as they captured 250 yards of enemy trench the Scots born Canadian was awarded yet another posthumous Victoria Cross for a Scot serving with the Canadian Expeditionary Forces.

While the war on land continued unabated in the Western Front and other minor fronts the naval war was fought wherever the German, Austrian or Turkish warships wished to operate. During the morning of 15 May 1917 Allied Drifters operating as a barrage across the Straits of Otranto were attacked by a squadron of Austrian Light Cruisers. The Cruisers each had taken a section of the barrage with a view to destroying this irritation for the enemy navy. The larger and vastly more heavily armed Cruisers had everything very much their own way at least until one of the enemy ships called upon one of the Drifters the "Gowanlea" to surrender. This small craft was skippered by Joseph Watt who originally came from Gardenstown in Banff, but was working as a fisherman out of Fraserburgh. When she was ordered to stop the "Gowanlea" was only 100 yards from the enemy ship. Instead of stopping as ordered Joseph Watt himself ordered full steam ahead, and called upon the crew to give three cheers as they prepared to fight to the death. The gun crew on the Drifter immediately engaged the enemy Cruiser and after firing only one shot a shell from the enemy disabled the "Gowanlea's" only gun. Under a very heavy and incessant fire from the enemy the crew worked to try and repair the gun. As the fishing boat tried to escape with fires burning the enemy Captain evidently thought the small boat was sinking and left the area. When the Cruiser was out of sight Skipper Watt took his boat along side the "Floandi" another of the victims of the Cruiser and removed the dead and injured. For his actions in the encounter with the Austrian Light Cruiser in the Straits of Otranto when 14 of the fleet of Drifters were sunk and many more damaged, including the "Gowanlea" Skipper Joseph Watt was decorated with the Country's highest award for gallantry.

Not all the action was taking place in France and Belgium as the British and Empire troops were still very much engaged on the Eastern Front with the Turks. The withdrawal from Gallipoli during December 1914 and January 1915 had strengthened the resolve of the Turks and it was not long before attempts were being made to cross the Suez Canal. By the middle of 1917 in Egypt the soldiers had settled into a trench warfare not dissimilar to that in France and Flanders except that instead of mud and rain it was sun and sand.

On 5 June some men of 1/4th Battalion of the Royal Scots Fusiliers were in an advanced post which had been rushed by the enemy. Second Lieutenant John Craig of that Battalion immediately organised a party to retake this post which had been lost. Having tracked the enemy back to their trench the Fusiliers set about removing the dead and wounded. Whilst they were busy at this work they came under rifle and machine gun fire. In this action one of the Company's Non Commissioned Officers had been wounded and way lying in full view of the enemy. A Medical Officer went out to the wounded man and he too was also wounded. Second Lieutenant Craig who was born in Comrie immediately went out to their assistance. He was successful in removing the soldier to safety in the British trench after which he again crossed the open ground and reached the wounded Medical Officer. Whilst returning to safety with the wounded officer Lieutenant Craig himself was wounded as the enemy poured intense fire across the ground in an effort to deter the rescue attempt. Both these rescues were carried out in broad daylight and in full view of a determined enemy. For his daring rescues of the 2 men Second Lieutenant Craig was awarded the Victoria Cross and became the only Scot to receive his medal for actions against the Turks in Egypt.

At 3.10am on the morning of 7 June 1917 the earth shook with such a force that tremors were felt almost 20 miles away. The tunnellers and miners of the British Army had placed beneath Messines Ridge a total of 20 mines and at that moment 19 of them exploded to herald the beginning of the battle which was to go down in history as the Battle of Passchendaele. Before the dust had settled the soldiers of Britain and her Empire were making their way slowly through the man made mist towards an enemy still shaking under the cover of another massive artillery barrage. Among those moving forward was Lance Corporal Samuel Frickleton (fig.11), who was born in Slamannan in Stirlingshire, but was serving in the 3rd Battalion of the New Zealand Infantry. As he moved forward at the head of his section into the barrage he personally destroyed an enemy machine gun which was causing casualties in the ranks of the advancing New Zealanders. As he continued to move further ahead he came across a second machine gun which he attacked and killed and complete crew of 12 men. As a result of him destroying the 2 machine guns there was no doubt that casualties had been prevented. These actions were carried out in spite of him having received a serious wound early on in the advance. This great example of heroism resulted in him being immediately promoted in the field and receiving the Victoria Cross. The only Scot to gain this award while serving in the New Zealand Forces.

The first phase of the Battle of Passchendaele was followed quickly by the second on the 31 July. The rain, mud and atrocious fighting conditions of the initial phase had become even more unpleasant as the fighting returned to the area around Ypres, where many thousands of men had died in the first 2 years of the war. When the barrage began on that day the men of the 51st (Highland) Division, including the 1/6th Battalion of the Gordon Highlanders were waiting expectantly on the ending of the barrage which signalled the entry into the battle of the Highlanders. The men of the 6th Gordons in the early stage of the attack quickly reached and captured their first objective. As they went about the work of consolidating their new position they came under a very accurate fire from a machine gun placement very close at hand. The Battalion which recruited many of its men from the Buckie area were pinned down by the firing from the gun and this prompted Private George McIntosh to rush towards the machine gun and throw Mills Bombs into the defended position. There is no doubt that the speed with which he reacted to the very dangerous situation took the enemy by complete surprise and in the process saved many lives. For his action in the advance at Ypres on a day in which his Regiment was to be almost decimated Buckie born Private McIntosh received a well deserved Victoria Cross. On this day the 1/6th Battalion of the Gordon Highlanders lost over 300 men and the award of the Victoria Cross to a member of the Battalion went some way to easing the pain of such a loss to the North East of Scotland.

The second Victoria Cross of the day to the Highland Division was won by Sergeant Alexander Edwards from Lossiemouth. Sergeant Edwards was leading a Company of his men from the 6th Battalion of the Seaforth Highlanders when their advance was held up by an enemy machine gun firing from a position in a wood. When the location of the post was established Sergeant Edwards led a small band of his men against it. The Sergeant himself was instrumental in the final capture of the gun and the killing of the crew. Later in the day when a well hidden sniper was causing many casualties amongst his men the soldier from Lossiemouth, although wounded in the arm himself crawled out and began to stalk the enemy. After a short while he was able to locate him and dispatch him without further loss to his men. By then all the officers except one had been killed or wounded and Sergeant Edwards realised that the success of the Battalion would depend on his men capturing the further most objective. Although he could have justified having himself removed from the line for medical attention he led the Seaforths against this last enemy trench. When the position was eventually captured the Scots Sergeant showed great skill in consolidating the captured ground. By his example and complete disregard for his personal safety the gallant Sergeant was able to win and hold valuable objectives which allowed his Battalion to succeed on this day. The brave Sergeant Edwards was eventually killed in action on 24 March 1918 east of Arras.

On that first day of the second phase of the Battle of Passchendaele a total of 14 Victoria Crosses were awarded to reflect the courage of those soldiers of Britain and her Empire who brought the Allies to the brink of victory in 1917.

As the Ypres phase of the Passchendaele continued more Scots were winning the Country's highest decoration for gallantry. The next Scot to win his Cross was Acting Company Sergeant Major John Skinner (fig.12) from Pollockshields in Glasgow. Sergeant Major Skinner had been in the army for more than 17 years and had fought in the war against the Boers where he had been wounded 3 times. When the war began in 1914 the Glasgow soldier was serving in the 1st Battalion of the King's Own Scottish Borderers and before he was killed in action at Vlamertinghe in Belgium in March 1918 he had been wounded a further 6 times. However on 18 August 1917 near Wijdendrift in Belgium his company was held up in its advance by concentrated machine gun fire. Although earlier wounded in the head he gathered up 6 men and with great skill and courage worked his way round some blockhouses from which the fire was coming. Being first on the scene he bombed the gun position and captured it single handed. He continued with his 6 men to the other 2 positions and cleared them of the enemy. He then returned to the relative safety of his Company's lines with 60 prisoners, 3 machine guns and 2 trench mortars. Company Sergeant Major who had already been decorated by the King with the Distinguished Conduct Medal for bravery in the early days of the war was now the proud recipient of the Victoria Cross.

The Battle of Passchendaele continued into November but before it ended 6 more Scots were to be decorated with the Country's highest award for gallantry. On 8 September Sergeant John Carmichael from Airdrie performed one of the most memorable acts of self sacrifice of the whole conflict. Sergeant Carmichael was working with men of the 9th battalion of the North Staffordshire Regiment in preparing and excavating a new trench system when he saw a hand grenade which had been dug up and was starting to burn. He at once rushed to the spot and as he went shouted a warning to the men standing nearby to make for cover. Although he could have thrown the bomb over the parapet he realised that this would endanger those men working above and outside the trench. Putting his steel helmet down to cover the bomb and reduce the effect of the blast he continued to shout warning to the men. When the grenade exploded he was blown out clear of the trench and severely injured. However no one else was even slightly injured as a result of his prompt reaction. For saving a situation which could so easily have ended in tragedy the brave Sergeant was decorated with the Victoria Cross to go along side the Military Medal he had won previously.

On the evening of 25 September and into the next morning men of the 1/9th Battalion of the Highland Light Infantry were defending trenches to the north of the Ypres to Menin road. The fighting was of such intensity that the men in the front line were beginning to run out of ammunition. Several times during the night and into the next morning when the lack of supply of ammunition was becoming a serious problem Acting Lance Corporal John Hamilton from Dumbarton collected bandoliers of ammunition and on his own initiative distributed them. Often in full view of enemy snipers and machine gunners Lance Corporal Hamilton went out whenever necessary to distribute his loads of ammunition. As a result of the good work done by the brave Lance Corporal the men of the Highland Light Infantry were able to hold their position against superior numbers of the enemy. For his cool courage at a time of great difficulty the brave Lance Corporal from Dumbarton was awarded a well deserved Victoria Cross.

Into October 1917 and there was still no sign of a break in the deadlock at Passchendaele. Another Scot to win the Victoria Cross for actions against enemy machine guns was Motherwell born Corporal William Clamp who was serving in the 6th Battalion of the Yorkshire Regiment. In circumstances similar to the previous Scottish winners Corporal Clamp's Regiment had been checked in their advance by enemy machine gun fire from concrete blockhouses. When the first of these was attacked Corporal Clamp and 2 of his men who had been wounded in the attempts were beaten back when they had been wounded. Having collected 2 more men and a supply of bombs the Corporal returned to the Blockhouse and hurled his bombs into the position. Many of the crew had been killed by the bombs and on entering he captured the gun and about 20 prisoners. Once he had returned with his valuable prizes he continued to encourage his men by displaying the greatest heroism until he was eventually killed by a snipers bullet to his head. For his outstanding gallantry on 9 October 1917 in the attacks on the concrete blockhouses Corporal Clamp was awarded a posthumous Victoria Cross.

On 26 October, just 17 days after the death of the brave Corporal Clamp and still during the continuing Passchendaele offensive Lieutenant Robert Shankland who was born in Saint Quivox near Ayr and who had emigrated to Canada in 1911 became the fourth Canadian Scot to win a Victoria Cross. Lieutenant Shankland who had already won the Distinguished Conduct Medal whilst serving in the ranks of the 43rd Battalion of the Manitoba Regiment, had rallied his men after they and remnants of other companies had been ordered to hold open ground in front of the hard pressed Germans. When the enemy made a counter attack which was repulsed he then communicated to headquarters an accurate and valuable report on the situation on the whole Brigade front. On returning to his men he continued to lead them with outstanding courage and inspiring example. As a reward for his leadership Lieutenant Shankland was awarded a much deserved Victoria Cross to be worn along side his Distinguished Conduct Medal.

A few days later the Canadian Expeditionary Force was still engaged around Passchendaele and this time another Canadian Scot serving in the 49th Battalion (Alberta Regiment) was also awarded the Victoria Cross. On 30 October the Canadians launched their attack against a strongly defended area of ground north of Meerscheele in Belgium. The advance was held up by determined resistance from the enemy and the men of the 49th Alberta Regiment came under a very heavy and accurate machine gun fire. Private Cecil Kinross who was born in Clackmannanshire, after he had made a careful survey of the surrounding area, removed all his excess equipment and was left with only his rifle and a bandolier of ammunition. Moving forward with the utmost care he crawled in broad daylight to a place where he knew the enemy machine gun post to be. When he felt that he was close enough to the enemy and still unseen he charged the final few yards and killed the crew of 6 men and destroyed the gun. By this act of individual courage his Battalion was able to establish itself in a very important position. The importance of Private Kinross's action on this day was reflected in the award of the Victoria Cross to yet another Canadian Scot.

On the same day and in the same area, Inverness born Lieutenant Hugh MacKenzie was in charge of a section of 4 machine guns manned by men of the 7th Company of the Canadian Machine Gun Corps. The officers of the Infantry Company they had been ordered to support had all become casualties with the result that the men were beginning to show signs of doubt in their own ability. On seeing this Lieutenant MacKenzie left a Corporal in charge of the machine guns and ran forward to rally the infantry. He then organised an attack and captured a pill-box which was causing some casualties amongst the infantrymen. He then led the frontal attack on the strong point and was instrumental in its final capture. However the brave Lieutenant who had already won a Distinguished Conduct Medal while still in the ranks was killed at the moment of the capture of the pill-box. For his work in reorganising the faltering infantry and leading them on to a successful conclusion in their attack the Lieutenant was awarded a posthumous Victoria Cross.

As the fighting around Passchendale continued into November 1917 yet another Canadian Scot won the supreme award for gallantry. At 6.00am on the 6 November the Canadians of the 1st Division attacked and occupied the hills to the north of the town of Passchendale. On the extreme left of the Canadian front, men of the 3rd Battalion of the 1st Central Ontario Regiment attacked Goudberg Spur. Guarding this spur was a heavily defended enemy machine gun post containing 6 guns. Time and time again the Ontario men attacked and were forced back by the murderous machine gun fire.

As the Canadians rose to attack, once again Corporal Colin Barron (who was born the illegitimate son of a soldier from Cullen, and himself born in Boyndie near Banff), crept around the flank and was causing enemy casualties with his Lewis gun. So accurate was his fire that he was able to capture an enemy machine gun which he then was able to turn on the fleeing Germans. This action produced far reaching results and allowed the Canadians to advance along the whole front and capture the spur. After the action he was promoted Sergeant and the award of the Victoria Cross was announced in the London Gazette on 11 January 1918.

In the early hours of 20 November 1917 history was being made as the massed tanks of the Royal Tank Corps moved forwards the marshalling areas to the front line. The static war which had been waged since the long past days of 1914 was suddenly about to burst into mobility. As the barrage ended the Battle of Cambrai began. It was not a coincidence that the area around the town of Cambrai was chosen as the stage from which the world would witness the entry of the tank into modern warfare. In this part of the front the landscape was one of chalk land which in comparison to the mud of Flanders was very dry and allowed the chance for the newly entered tanks to perform in the way that they had been designed. So in the morning of Tuesday 20 November the 216 tanks were in the front to begin the third stage of the battle which had begun on 31 July at Passchendaele. All along the front the advance had moved virtually without resistance, except in that part of the line occupied by men of the 51st (Highland) Division. Around the village of Flesquieres the Highlanders floundered and became easy targets for a nest of enemy machine guns. These guns were causing many casualties amongst the men of the 5th Battalion of the Seaforth Highlanders. It was decided that a Lewis gun was needed to deal with the troublesome enemy gunners. Kinlochbervie man Lance Corporal Robert McBeath volunteered to work the Lewis gun. Moving off alone armed only with the gun and a revolver he quickly located one of the enemy guns from its muzzle flash. When he got within range he swiftly dispatched the gunner with his revolver. When he had located the positions of the other guns he enlisted the help of a tank in the line and directing fire for the tank crew forced the enemy gunners to go to ground in a deep dugout. Without a moments hesitation Lance Corporal McBeath followed them into the shelter and shot the first man who challenged him. At this point the rest of the enemy including 3 officers and 30 men surrendered. Inside the dugout there was a further 5 machine guns which the gallant Lance Corporal destroyed before returning to his own lines with his prisoners. As a result of his courage in destroying the opposition and thus allowing the advance to proceed Lance Corporal McBeath was decorated with the Victoria Cross.

The first day of the Battle of Cambrai produced the 8th Canadian Scottish winner of the Victoria Cross, Lieutenant Harcus Strachan an Officer in the Fort Garry Horse. Although born in Bo'ness he had emigrated to Canada in 1905 after he bought a farm in Alberta. At Masnieres to the south of where the Highland Division had failed Lieutenant Strachan was left in command of a squadron of his Regiment as it was approaching the German front line at a pace little short of a gallop. Without a moments hesitation he led his men across the first line of machine guns and with the survivors continued on to charge an enemy artillery battery. Lieutenant Strachan personally killed 7 of the enemy artillery men with his sword. Having silenced the battery he gathered up his men and with 15 prisoners made his way aback almost 2 miles to the original British lines, after having had to stampede the horses and make their way back on foot. On the way back this small bank of horseless cavalry encountered the enemy on 4 occasions and each time had to fight a rearguard action through to their own lines without further loss to any of the men. For his charge reminiscent of Balaclava the Lieutenant who had already won the Military Cross in the previous May was awarded an outstanding Victoria Cross.

One week after the tanks had moved into the front line their influence was starting to wane. The 51st (Highland) Division had regained some of its pride which had been dented at Flesquieres earlier and were by then pressing hard on the outskirts of Fontaine-Notre-Dame, when they were relieved by the Guards Division and on 27 November a concentrated effort was made in the area of the town. Accompanied by some 30 tanks the Guards engaged the enemy and started to sustain many casualties. The early successes of the Guard were soon wiped out by a determined counter attack by the Germans. Just prior to the counter attack developing Sergeant John McAulay of the 1st Battalion of the Scots Guards, who had been a police Sergeant in the Northern Division of the Glasgow Police, had organised the remnants of his Company and successfully repulsed the early German attempts to remove the Guardsmen. When he noticed the enemy massing for a more determined counter attack he again organised his men and with skilful use of the remaining machine guns caused many casualties amongst the enemy. Realising that the situation was becoming desperate he carried his Company Commander who had been mortally wounded, a great distance to a place of safety. Whilst carrying his Officer to safety he was twice intercepted by the enemy and on each occasion he was forced to kill them in order to escape. For his conduct throughout this day the Gallant Glasgow Policeman was awarded a Victoria Cross which he wore along side the Distinguished Conduct Medal he had won at Ypres on 31 July, 4 months earlier.

As the battles around the Cambrai Salient continued the Germans were able to launch another even more determined counter attack on the last day of November. The speed of the German advance on this day was so fast that many British Battalions were quickly surrounded as the front seemed to collapse under the weight of the enemy numbers. In the part of the front near Gonnelieu amongst those surrounded was "C" Battery of 63rd Brigade, Royal Field Artillery, which had been reduced to 5 men after the loss of the Battery Commander and 5 Sergeants. The only officer left was Temporary Lieutenant Samuel Wallace from Thornhill in Dumfriesshire. Lieutenant Wallace maintained the firing of the guns by bringing the tails closer together to allow one man to perform several of the tasks required to keep them firing. This makeshift arrangement allowed the guns to keep up their firing rate for 8 hours. Finally due to exhaustion of his men and the fact that infantry support had arrived allowed the guns to be abandoned. In spite of the tiredness of the men this was an orderly withdrawal and all the essential parts of the guns were removed as were all the wounded from the Battery. As a result of his outstanding leadership and personal courage Lieutenant Wallace was decorated with the Victoria Cross. The guns which were abandoned were later recovered and the missing parts returned to enable them to complete the valuable work started by the gallant Lieutenant and his Gunners.

The next Scot to win the Victoria Cross was Acting Captain George Paton from Innellan near Dunoon in Argyllshire. On 1 December also at Gonnelieu a unit on the left flank of Captain Paton's position was being driven back and causing men of his battalion the 4th Grenadier Guards to be practically surrounded. Taking charge of the situation he fearlessly walked up and down the line within 50 yards of the enemy who were showering the position with intense rifle fire, readjusting the line as required. He personally removed several wounded men before he himself left the position. Later in the day when he had again set up defensive positions in the line his men were counter attacked on 4 occasions and each time Captain Paton established himself on the parapet to direct his men. When the enemy had broken through on his flank he and 4 others mounted the parapet and by their accurate fire forced the enemy to withdraw. Later in the day still defending this position he was killed. For his actions throughout this day the gallant Captain became the first Grenadier Officer since the Crimean War to win a Victoria Cross albeit posthumously.

The last Scot to win the Country's highest decoration for bravery in 1917 was Second Lieutenant Stanley Boughey of the 1/4th Battalion of the Royal Scots Fusiliers. The Turks were still in occupation of Palestine although British and Empire troops were beginning to gain control. On 1 December the same day as Captain Paton was killed in winning his Victoria Cross on the Western Front, Ayrshire born Lieutenant Boughey was in trenches being attacked by Turkish soldiers using automatic rifles and bombs. The Turks had managed to crawl to within 30 yards of the Scots Fusiliers trenches. Realising the immediate danger Second Lieutenant Boughey rushed forward alone carrying bombs right up to the enemy with such determination that a party of 30 surrendered. After he had secured, as he thought his prisoners he was shot and fatally wounded by one of them as he returned for more bombs. This gallant Officer died from his wound 3 days later and was awarded a posthumous Victoria Cross.

As the winter of 1917 moved into the spring of 1918 the Allied Commanders were beginning to suspect a massive offensive all along the length of the front as the defences in the Hindenburg Line had not been breached to any great extent.

By the middle of March men who were veterans of the trenches were beginning to sense that a great battle was about to be fought. Raids into the Allied lines were taking place on a very regular basis and these were construed, rightly so, as information gathering sorties. The attack was expected on 21 March and no one in the British trenches was taken by surprise when at 5am began the greatest artillery barrage the war had known when over 6,500 German guns opened fire in unison. Three hours later the majority of the enemy's guns were still bombarding the British front and the concentrations of troops behind the forward trenches. At 9.30am, four and a half hours after the German barrage began the enemy infantry in tens of thousands went over the top and very soon afterwards were making their way along the British trench systems.

East of the village of Marteville men of the 8th Battalion of the Argyll and Sutherland Highlanders had been experiencing some of the enemy's most accurate shelling and had as a result sustained many casualties. Amongst the many wounded was Alloa born Second Lieutenant John Buchan of the 7th Battalion who was attached to the 8th. He had been wounded early on in the bombardment and refused to go to the rear for treatment for his wounds and instead elected to remain with the men of his platoon. When the shelling was at its height he visited, with complete disregard to his gun safety, all the posts of his men and encouraged them to withstand the fearful pounding which they were taking. Later when the enemy were creeping close to the position and raking the area with machine gun fire he continued to encourage all his men even though he himself had sustained another wound. As the enemy were advancing with such speed he noticed that his position was almost surrounded and then he gathered up what was left of his men with a view to making a fighting withdrawal to the British lines. When the German Commander called upon him to surrender he replied by leading his men as they fought their way through the surrounding German troops. He quickly established a new position and held out until dusk against determined attacks from the enemy. Due to a mix up back in the British lines this small band were not ordered to withdraw and again found themselves surrounded. Second Lieutenant Buchan was last seen defending this position against overwhelming odds. The gallantry and self sacrifice of this Officer over 2 days of some of the most desperate fighting seen in the Western Front resulted in yet another posthumous Victoria Cross to a Scottish born soldier.

On the same day as second Lieutenant Buchan was winning his decoration Edinburgh born Lieutenant Allan Ker was winning his at Saint Quentin. Again the enemy in massed numbers had broken through the British line. When the enemy were pressing hard Lieutenant Ker with just 1 machine gun succeeded in holding up the German advance and was causing many casualties. This gallant Officer then remained at his post with several of his men who had been badly wounded and personally beat off several bayonet attacks with his revolver after the machine gun had been destroyed. In spite of his exhaustion from the fighting and gas poisoning Lieutenant Ker only surrendered after he had used all ammunition and the post had been overrun. He had managed to hold off over 500 of the enemy for more than 3 hours. For his conspicuous gallantry on this day the Gordon Highlander who had been attached to the 61st Battalion of the Machine Gun Corps was awarded a well deserved Victoria Cross after he had returned from being a prisoner of war in Germany.

The next award for action during the Ludendorff Offensive went to Glasgow born Acting Lieutenant Colonel William Anderson who was in command of the 12th Battalion of the Highland Light Infantry. On 25 March 1918 at Bois Favieres near Maricourt, where the enemy had entered into a wood and were pressing the flank of the Highland Light Infantry, and fearing that such an infiltration would be endanger the complete flank of his Battalion Lieutenant Colonel Anderson gathered together the 2 remaining Companies of his men and counter attacked the Germans forcing them to abandon the wood. In this action he was instrumental in the capture of 12 machine guns and some 70 prisoners. Later in the same day after the enemy had taken up position in an abandoned timber yard about 300 yards from an important village he organised his men in preparation for a counter attack which he lead in person and throughout he showed complete disregard for his own safety. This counter attack drove the enemy from its position but unfortunately as he lead his men Lieutenant Colonel Anderson was killed fighting among the enemy in defended positions. Within 2 months of his death the London Gazette carried the citation for the award of the Victoria Cross to the gallant Commanding Officer of the 12th Battalion of the Highland Light Infantry.

Ever since that massive bombardment on 21 March the Ludendorff Offensive had tried in vain on several occasions to drive a wedge between the British and French Armies. The last of these offenses which started on 15 July became known as the Second Battle of the Marne. The initial assault started as had the previous ones with success, however this time the Allies aided by men of the American Expeditionary Force counter attacked on 18 July and 2 days later were joined by 2 further Divisions, one British and one American.

During this final attempt by the Germans the 51st (Highland) Division was in support of the French Army around the River Ardre. On 20 July near Marfaux in the Ardre valley the advance of the 4th Battalion of the Seaforth Highlanders was being held up by deadly accurate machine gun fire. When the Seaforths could advance no further Nitshill, near Glasgow born Sergeant John Meikle (fig.14) on his own initiative attacked across 150 yards of open ground armed only with a revolver and a heavy stick. When he came on the machine gun post he emptied the revolver into the crews of the 2 guns and put the rest out of action with his heavy stick. He then stood up and waved his comrades on. A short while later another machine gun was holding up progress for the Seaforths. Angered by the fact that most of his platoon had now become casualties he picked up a rifle and bayonet from a fallen comrade and charged the offending gun. When he was almost on top of the gun he fell back dead. However his bravery had spurred on his men and they following close behind him, overpowered the crew and destroyed the gun. For his courage in removing the menace of the guns which were causing casualties amongst his men Sergeant Meikle who had won the Military Medal earlier in the war was decorated posthumously with the Victoria Cross.

At the beginning of August 1918 the front line almost reached the town of Amiens and in the period up to 11 August the British in their sector had pushed the enemy 5 miles nearer the defensive Siegfried line. In 4 days of fierce fighting the men of the 78th Battalion of the Manitoba Regiment (Winnipeg Grenadiers) had their advance checked by intense and accurate enemy machine gun fire. Lieutenant James Tait who originally came from a village called Greenbrae in Dumfriesshire and had already won a Military Cross in the fighting to secure Vimy Ridge in 1917 was in command of a Company which was losing many men to this murderous fire. He led his men forward under a hail of bullets until they could advance no further. Alone he moved out of cover and made his way towards the gun position from which his men were receiving even more casualties. When he killed the enemy gunner he inspired his men to follow his example and they attacked more of the machine gun posts. As a result of this a further

12 machine guns were captured, along with 20 prisoners. Having removed the menace of the guns he began to consolidate his hard won position. The enemy realising the importance of this newly gained ground bombarded the Canadians for many hours. It was during this period that the Canadian Scot displayed outstanding courage and even after he had been seriously wounded he continued to direct his men until he died on 11 August. For his conspicuous gallantry over the 3 days when his Company was under such intense bombardment from the enemy and for his example in attacking and eliminating the enemy machine gun post this gallant Officer was awarded yet another posthumous Victoria Cross for a Canadian Scot.

The next Scot to win the Victoria Cross was described in a letter to his parents in Linwood from his Commanding Officer on the occasion of the notification of his death as being "one of the bravest boys in the Battalion, in fact the bravest I have ever known". This boy was Private Hugh McIver (fig.15) of the 2nd Battalion of the Royal Scots. Private McIver had volunteered for the Army in August 1914 and before he died on 2 September 1918 he had been decorated 3 times, the Victoria Cross and the Military Medal twice. It was on 23 August that Private McIver, when he was the Company Runner at Courcelles-le-Comte near Bapaume, performed the deed which won for him the Country's highest award for gallantry. At a time when his Company was suffering as the result of a very accurate machine gun fire he continued to carry messages regardless of his own safety. On one occasion he pursued an enemy scout into a machine gun nest and killed 6 of the garrison, captured 20 prisoners and 2 guns before returning to his own lines. By his action his Company was able to proceed without further loss. Later in the day when he noticed that a British tank was directing fire at british Infantry from a very close range he was able to attract the attention of the tank gunner and prevent him from inflicting more injuries on his own men. By his courage on this day the Linwood born soldier saved the lives of many of his comrades. Private McIver never did not know that he had been awarded the Victoria Cross as he was killed in action just 10 days later and is buried in the Vraucourt Copse British Cemetery north east of Bapaume. King George V presented his Cross to his proud but sad parents as a special ceremony in Buckingham Palace on 13 February 1919.

As the fighting to break through the Siegfried defences continued the men of the 1/6th Battalion of the Highland Light Infantry were under the continuous bombardment from enemy artillery and machine gunners. The acting Adjutant of the Highland Light Infantry was Islay born Temporary Lieutenant David MacIntyre (fig.16) of the Argyll and Sutherland Highlanders. During the days from 24 to 27 August the courage of this Officer was very much in evidence as he was in command of the firing line occupied by his adopted Regiment. Protecting the enemy machine guns was strong wire defences and Lieutenant MacIntyre personally made himself aware of all aspects of the entanglements. At a place where the wire was particularly strong he led out his men to make gaps in it. A short time later when the greater part of the line was being held up by enemy machine guns he rallied his men and attacked them. The gunners immediately left their guns and made for what they considered the safety of a pill box. Following the gunners into the stronghold Lieutenant MacIntyre had his men captured an officer 10 other ranks and 5 machine guns. From this position he led attacks on 3 more pill boxes and captured them thus enabling his Battalion to capture an important section of the front. When the Battalion was ordered to take up a defensive position Lieutenant MacIntyre was ordered to rest away from the front, before he was able to go to the rear as he was surveying an exposed flank an enemy machine gun opened fire and without a moments hesitation he left his trench and charged the gun putting the crew to flight. As the success of the advance was largely due to this gallant Officers initiative and leadership the minister's son was decorated with a most deserved Victoria Cross.

Before August was ended the ninth Canadian Scot was decorated with the Victoria Cross. He was Lieutenant Colonel William Clark-Kennedy of the 24th Battalion of the Quebec Regiment, a Scot who had emigrated to Canada in 1903 after he had seen service in the Boer War where he had been Mentioned in Despatches. In April 1915 at the Second Battle of Ypres he was decorated by the French with the Croix de Guerre (with Palms) and a month later at the Battle of Festubert he received his first Distinguished Service Order. His second Distinguished Service Order was awarded for bravery on the Somme in August 1918. Thus by the end of the same month he was highly decorated and experienced soldier. On 27th August 1918 at the front line between Fresnes and Rouvroy the Brigade of which

Lieutenant Colonel Clark-Kennedy's Battalion was a mainstay was suffering many casualties. When this was at its height the Canadian Scot encouraged his men and led them forward, at the same time controlling those Battalions on either side of his, thus enabling the whole Brigade from to advance. On the next day he, by his prominence, inevitably received a serious wound. Despite pain and severe loss of blood he insisted on remaining with his men until his Battalion had won a position from which the advance could be resumed. For his outstanding leadership on the 27 and 28 August the Canadian who was born in Dunskey in Wigtonshire was decorated with the Victoria Cross.

The month of August had not quite finished when another Scots born soldier won the Victoria Cross. He was Second Lieutenant James Huffam who, born in Dunblane in Perthshire, was serving in the 2nd Battalion of the Duke of Wellington's (West Riding) Regiment. On the last day of the month at Saint Servin's Farm when his Company came under repeated fire from an enemy machine gun Lieutenant Huffam accompanied by 3 of his men rushed the offending gun and quickly put it out of action, at the same time capturing 8 of the enemy. The Germans seemed to take exception to this and immediately launched an attack of such ferocity that the men of the Duke of Wellington's Regiment had to conduct a fighting retreat during which Lieutenant Huffam carried a wounded man to the new defensive line. Later in the same day another enemy machine gun was encountered and was holding up the advance. This time the Scots Lieutenant and 2 men went out and captured the gun and brought in prisoners and thus allowed the advance to continue without excessive casualties.

As the operations to smash the defences on the Hindenburg Line continued in the hope that it would bring the war to a speedy conclusion, the men of the 1/5th Battalion of the Highland Light Infantry were in action north east of Moeuvres. On 16 September they found an enemy who was determined not to lose any more ground and even hoping to gain ground. The supply of troops to Ludendorff's Army was beginning to end and the Germans were now having to commit untrained men and boys to battle. The men of the Highland Light Infantry had been detailed to relieve another Battalion in the from line and Corporal David Hunter from Dunfermline was ordered to establish himself in some shell holes very close to the enemy trenches. As the changeover had taken place in darkness he had no opportunity to get to know the surrounding countryside. Early in the following morning the enemy counter attacked and overran the posts on either flank of Corporal Hunter and his section, which resulted in him being surrounded. Although short of food and water he was determined to hold his ground at all costs. On the evening of his second day in isolation he tried to contact his Company without success. The enemy launched several attacks during the day and night in an effort to try and dislodge the Corporal and his section and each time they were driven back by the accurate fire of the defenders. After over 48 hours without food or water this gallant band was relieved. During this time the position held by Corporal Hunter and his men was bombarded by the Germans and by virtue of its place within the enemy lines was also bombarded by the British. For the outstanding bravery and determination, not forgetting endurance Corporal Hunter was decorated with a well deserved Victoria Cross.

The knot around the neck of the Germans was gradually tightening and at last Britain and her Allies could see an end to the war.

On 28 September a mixed force of Belgians and British opened up on a front stretching from Dixmunde in the north to Ploegsteert in the south a distance of 20 miles. In the northern part of the front there was a prelude to the battle in the usual form of a massive artillery bombardment lasting several hours whereas in the south there was no warning of the attack to come. The successes on this day were almost immediate as both the Belgians in the north and the British in the south moved ahead with a gathering momentum. In the fighting to gain the crest of the ridge at Wytschaete men of the 1/5th Battalion of the King's Own Scottish Borderers encountered several enemy dugouts as they advanced towards Piccadilly Farm. It was here that Acting Sergeant Louis McGuffie (fig.17) entered into several of these and captured many prisoners. When his Battalion was consolidating this newly won position Sergeant McGuffie went out into No-Man's-Land in pursuit of Germans who were intent in slipping back to their own lines. Whilst he was out he came across a group of British, who were being led into captivity. He rescued them and led back to the safety of the British lines. Later in the day while in command of a platoon he again rounded up prisoners and brought them back. Unfortunately this gallant Non Commissioned Officer from Wigtown was killed by a shell in the fighting around Wytschaete on 4 October. Sergeant McGuffie died in action before it was announced that he had been awarded the Victoria Cross.

By now the situation in the German held town of Cambrai was becoming quite serious. The Canadians were in the midst of some extremely fierce fighting around the town. It was in this sector of the front that the last Canadian Scot performed with such distinction that he was decorated with the Victoria Cross. He was Temporary Captain John MacGregor from Nairn. Captain MacGregor had enlisted in the Canadian Mounted Rifles in March 1915 and had made his way through the ranks after having won a Distinguished Conduct Medal as well as a Military Cross and Bar before winning his Victoria Cross. Captain MacGregor serving in the 2nd Canadian Mounted Rifles of the 1st Central Ontario Regiment came under intense fire from the enemy on 29 September and was wounded early on in the attack. Although hindered by his wound he led his Company to locate and put out of action enemy machine guns which were holding up the advance. When he located the nest he rushed forward in broad daylight alone across ground swept by intense rifle and machine gun fire, armed only with a rifle and bayonet and succeeded in killing 4 of the enemy and capturing a further 8. By his swift action many of his men were prevented from becoming casualties in the advance which was then allowed to continue. After regrouping his men he continued to give support to troops on his flanks. Also at a time when the enemy were showing stubborn resistance he went out amongst his men with complete disregard for his own safety and organised them when they met with difficult opposition. Later as the advance continued he carried out alone a reconnaissance under heavy fire to establish the strength of the enemy at Neuville Saint Remy before entering the village with his men. This move greatly assisted the advance on the sector of the front at Tilloy. Throughout the period 29 September to 3 October Captain MacGregor displayed the greatest bravery and leadership.

On 14 October the war which had begun on 22 August 1914 entered into what would be its last month. All along the front the Allies were advancing into new areas which up to then had been unaffected by the ravages of war. Although the weather had changed from the dryness of the European summer to the wetness of an early winter the Allies were making good progress in their advance.

On this day men of the Royal Engineers were maintaining a cork float bridge across the Canal de la Sensee near Aubencheul-au-Bac which was under a very intense machine gun fire. In the morning when the Infantry were crossing the temporary bridge to engage the enemy entrenched on the other side it began to break up. On seeing this Corporal James McPhie from Edinburgh, serving with 416th (Edinburgh) Field Company of the Royal Engineers jumped into the water and tried to hold the cork and wood together by hand. When this failed he swam back and returned with material to effect a repair. Although it was by then daylight and under a close and attentive fire from the enemy he was able to make a repair. having done this he with an axe in his hand led the Infantry across the bridge. While he was on the bridge he was shot and fell into the water, from which he clambered back onto the deck of the bridge where he was shot several more times as he tried to lead the Infantry across to the enemy. In recognition of his courage and determination at such a critical time the Territorial Corporal from Edinburgh was decorated with a posthumous Victoria Cross.

The next Scot to win the decoration was Sergeant John O'Neill from Airdrie who was at the time serving in the 2nd Battalion of the Prince of Wales' Leinster Regiment. Sergeant O'Neill and his Company had been halted in there advance near Moorseele in Belgium by 2 machine guns and an enemy Field Battery firing over open sights. Although at the head of 11 men only he charged the battery and captured 4 field guns, 2 machine guns and 16 prisoners. Also on the morning of 20 October he along with another man rushed an enemy machine gun post and in the attack caused over 100 of the enemy to flee. For his remarkable courage and leadership which he displayed during the operations around Moorseele Sergeant John O'Neill who had already won the British and French Military Medals was decorated with the Victoria Cross.

Also on 20 October at Solesmes near Cambrai Acting Sergeant John Daykins from Ormiston in Roxburghshire was in charge of the remaining 12 men of his platoon when they were attacked by a

German machine gun firing from a position near the church in the village. By prompt action he and his men were able to rush the post and during the vicious hand to hand fighting which ensued Sergeant Daykins killed many of the enemy himself and secured the position in addition to capturing 30 prisoners. He then located another machine gun which was holding up some of his Company and alone he made his way towards it. Very shortly afterwards he was seen returning with 25 prisoners and a machine gun, which was later mounted in the British line and was put to good use in repelling the enemy attacks. For his magnificent fighting spirit and inspiration to his men this gallant soldier was awarded the Victoria Cross.

The fighting was now almost entirely in Belgium and the German resistance was crumbling fast in all directions allowing the Allied Armies to advance over greater distances than they had moved in the whole of the fighting in the Western Front.

On 22 October at Hoogemolen Lieutenant David McGregor was in command of machine guns which were to be used to support his Battalion, the 6th Royal Scots, when they made the assault on the enemy lines. His guns were hidden in a sunken road which was under the full observation of the enemy, for as soon as they moved they were subjected to a very accurate fire. Lieutenant McGregor ordered the guns to take a safer route and he then ordered the driver of his limber to gallop across 600 yards of open ground while he way lying flat on it to a place from which he could direct his guns. Once having crossed the ground under such an intense enfilade in which the driver and all the horses were wounded he continued to direct the fire for his gunners until he was killed as he directed fired onto a trench mortar battery. For his gallantry in getting his guns into action to support the Royal Scots Lieutenant McGregor who was born in Edinburgh was awarded the last posthumous Victoria Cross for a Scots born soldier in the Great War.

However Lieutenant McGregor was not the last Scot to win a Victoria Cross and the next award was made to Lieutenant William Bissett of the 1/6th Battalion of the Argyll and Sutherland Highlanders, who on 25 October, when his platoon had been in action east of Maing in France, had assumed command after all the Officers had become casualties. After a determined counter attack had turned his left flank he was forced to withdraw to a railway. The enemy continued its advance when the Highlanders ran our of ammunition. Then Lieutenant Bissett mounted the embankment and called on his men to fix bayonets and charge. This they did and drove the greater numbers of the enemy ahead of them to a place where he was able to establish a new defensive position. For his example of courage and leadership at a critical time in the attack the Crieff born Officer who had enlisted at the outbreak of war as a Private soldier was awarded the Victoria Cross.

On the last day of October the fighting was centred on the town of Audenarde in Belgium where Carluke born sergeant Thomas Caldwell was serving with the 12th Battalion of the Royal Scots Fusiliers. Sergeant Caldwell was in command of a Lewis gun section which was engaged in clearing a farmhouse. When his section came under intense fire from a very close range and coming from the direction of a nearby farmhouse Sergeant Caldwell rushed towards the farm and in spite of the intensity of the rifle fire reached the enemy position which he captured single handed and returned with 18 prisoners. By his determined attack on this position he removed a serious obstacle to the advance and as a result also prevented many casualties. For his example of fearless courage this Scottish soldier also earned a well deserved Victoria Cross.

Just as in 1914 the first 2 awards of the Victoria Cross to Scots went to men serving in the Royal Engineers as did the last 2 awards to Scots in the Great War.

The first of these on 4 November went to Sapper Adam Archibald from Leith who was serving in the 218th Field Company near Ors in France when yet another canal had to be crossed in the advance towards Germany. The party in which Sapper Archibald was employed was building a floating bridge to allow Infantry to cross in order to engage the enemy dug in on the other bank. He was very prominent in the work which was being carried out under heavy artillery and machine gun fire. The machine gunners were concentrating on the Sapper as he was working with the cork floats. In spite of the attention from the enemy he continued to work towards the completion of the bridge. The supreme devotion to duty of Sapper Archibald who collapsed from gas poisoning as he completed the work resulted in him being awarded the Victoria Cross.

The last award to a Scot in the Great war was also won on the same day at another canal crossing. This time the fighting was across the Sambre-Oise Canal at one of the locks 2 miles south of Catillon. Acting Major George Findlay was leading the bridging and assault parties when they came under a severe fire which was causing many casualties. When the work was halted due to this fire Major Findlay gathered up the remnants of his men and returned to try and repair the bridges. At the third attempt he managed to have a bridge placed across the canal and he himself was the first man across. He remained directing his men until all the necessary repair work had been completed. It was due to Major Findlay's gallantry and devotion to duty that this very important crossing was established and for this work the Major from Balloch in Loch Lomondside became the last Scot to be decorated with the Victoria Cross in the Great War.

On the morning of 11 November 1918 Britain and her Allies ceased to be at war with Germany and great crowds were out in force all over the Empire as well as in Scotland to celebrate the end of the war to end all wars. A war which had left a total of over 8,500,000 dead on both sides and over 21,000,000 who had been wounded.

Of the 633 Victoria Crosses awarded during the Great War a total of 73 were won by Scottish born soldiers and sailors serving in the armies of almost all of the countries of the Empire.

IRAQ 1920

Although the great war had ended and the divisions of the Middle East had been completed the Allies were still not sure what was happening in the former Ottoman Empire. Turkey had been defeated along with Germany and Austria but seemed to be carrying on as she had done before the war. By the early months of 1920 it became apparent that the defeated Turks were experiencing violence as an early day event and atrocities were not uncommon.

As part of the division of the former Turkey France would administer Syria and Britain was to have mandates over Palestine and Mesopotamia. A situation which made it ripe for a nationalist movement led by Mustapha Kemel to flourish. By 22 June 1920 the Turks were back at war as the Arabs had taken advantage of the unrest and revolted in a move towards independence. In Mesopotamia soldiers who had fought in the campaigns of the Great War were now engaged in suppressing the revolt of the Arabs. On the evening of 24 July 1920 about 15 miles from Hillah a Company of men from the 2nd Battalion of the Manchester Regiment were in the command of Captain George Henderson from East Gordon in Berwickshire. Captain Henderson who had twice been awarded the Distinguished Service Order and a Military Cross had been ordered to retire and when he was doing so his men were fired upon by a large number of Arabs. In the panic which ensued the men of the Manchesters began to waver. On seeing this Captain Henderson immediately reorganised his men and led them into the attack and drove off the enemy. On 2 more occasions he led his men with fixed bayonets against the enemy forcing them to retreat. At this time of great danger and with the threat of panic from his men he took control and rallied them. During a later charge he was wounded but refused to leave his command to have his wound attended to. As he was about to enter the objective this Officer was wounded yet again only this time fatally. When he realised he could do no more he asked to be propped up on the embankment to see the fighting. There he died. For his gallantry and leadership Captain Henderson was awarded a posthumous Victoria Cross.

Of the 5 awards made for actions between the Great War and the Second World War 4 of these were posthumous with one for the gallant Scot who died in Mesopotamia.

THE SECOND WORLD WAR 1939/45

After the ravages of the static war of 1914 to 1919 the world careered towards the most mobile war ever fought. Just 15 years after the Treaty of Versailles had been signed to end the carnage of 5 years of war the like of which the world had never known it seemed unlikely that the world would see another on such a scale. The main antagonists were all now members of the League of Nations which was set up to react if aggression was to raise its ugly head anywhere in the world.

In 1931 Japan a member of the League attacked China and the rest of the world stood back to await the outcome. Mussolini the Italian leader was also taking a keen interest in the events in the far east. Realising that the League of Nations was powerless to stop any would-be aggressor he developed his own ideas for a New Roman Empire. In 1935 his ambitions in Africa led to the invasion of Abyssinia, which was situated in between the Italian colonies of Eritrea and Somaliland. Again the worlds police force stood by powerless as the Emperor of Abyssinia Haile Selassie was forced into an exile from where he appealed for help from the League of Nations to get the Italians out of his Country. The League did respond and imposed trade sanctions against Italy. However these sanctions only served to strengthen the alliance between the Italian leader and Adolph Hitler, the German leader. By this time Hitler himself had realised just how weak the League was and soon saw his chance in the Civil War in Spain. Both Mussolini and Hitler sent their troops into Spain in support of General Franco in his struggle against the Spanish Government. On the other hand Russia sent help to the Spanish Government. Other countries including Britain cautions in case another World War would result, did nothing.

By 1938 Hitler felt that the time was right to re-affirm his position and marched into Austria and announced to the rest of the world that she was now part of the German Reich. In September 1918 the British Prime Minister Neville Chamberlain flew to Germany to meet with Hitler and he hoped to persuade him to keep the peace. Hitler had expressed the desire to encompass all those areas, where German speaking people were living, into the Great German Reich. In particular he had shown interest in that part of Czechoslovakia known as the Sudetenland, an area along the border with Germany. In order to maintain peace in Europe the leaders including Chamberlain, meeting in Munich agreed that Hitler and Germany could have what was desired, in return for a promise of peace. Within 6 months Hitler showed to the rest of the world just what his promise had meant when he invaded the remainder of Czechoslovakia. Now the German leader had shown his true ambition, these people were not Germans and no nation in Europe could consider itself safe from his territorial plundering.

After the announcement of the inclusion of the whole of Czechoslovakia into the growing German Reich Hitler turned his attention to demanding the return of the Polish Corridor and the Baltic seaport of Danzig.

As this time Britain and France signed a treaty with Poland whereby they would defend her in event of aggression from her eastern or western borders. Britain tried to negotiate with the Russia but Stalin, the Russian leader, had already signed a Non-Aggression Pact with Germany. Thus Hitler was able to invade Poland on 1 September 1939 with the knowledge that the Russians would not enter into the fight.

Britain and France immediately demanded the withdrawal of all German forces from Poland. Hitler refused and on Sunday 3 September 1939 Britain and France declared war on Germany for the second time in 25 years. On the same day air raid sirens were heard in Scotland and many people went into air raid shelters not for the last time.

After 3 weeks the Germans had all but overrun Poland. In the west the massed armies of France and Germany faced each other from 2 lines of concrete forts, the French in the Maginot Line and the Germans in the Siegfreid Line.

There then followed a period which the Americans referred to as "the phoney war", during which there was no real fighting while both sides were sizing each other up. In April 1940 this phase of the war came to an end when German forces attacked and quickly overcame both Norway and Denmark, neither country having declared war, and both keen to remain neutral in the war. Rather belatedly the British tried to gain a foothold in Norway from which they were soon forced to withdraw.

The following month the Germans attacked the Low Countries, Holland and Belgium after having moved around the northern end of the Maginot Line. The British Expeditionary Force like their 1914 namesakes moved north to meet the oncoming German army. This small force was no match for the highly mechanised Germans and were quickly, as in 1914, on the retreat. Left with only one way of escape the B.E.F. moved north towards the coast in the hope they would be rescued at the sea. It was only a miracle which could save them and only a miracle did as over 350,000 men of the British Expeditionary Force were snatched from the shores at Dunkirk, by many hundreds of little ships which had left many of the English south coast ports with one thing in mind, the rescue of the B.E.F.

Although the main force had been rescued the men of the 51st (Highland) Division had been forced to fight on further to the west, where, as they made there way to the coast, the main part of the Division was surrounded at the French town of St.Valery. After much desperate fighting the major part of this Highland Division was forced to surrender. Part of this Division did manage to reach the sea and escape to form the nucleus of the reformed 51st (Highland) Division which performed so well in North Africa and beyond to Berlin itself.

With the fall of France Britain stood alone against the might of the German war machine. They were the masters of Europe although they were far from masters over Europe. The Royal Air Force was still able to carry the war into Germany and the Luftwaffe soon realised that they alone could not bring Britain to her knees. It was during one of these raids deep into the heart of enemy occupied Europe that a young man from Paisley wrote his name in the history of air warfare. On 15 September 1940 after returning from a successful raid on German barges the Hampden Bomber in which Sergeant John Hannah (fig.18) was the wireless operator and air gunner was subjected to an intense anti-aircraft bombardment in the skies over the Belgian town of Antwerp. During this attack the plane was hit in several placed which caused fires which spread so quickly that the rear gunner and the navigator baled out. Although he could have done likewise Sergeant Hannah opted to remain with the pilot and started to fight the fires with the in-flight fire extinguishers. When these were exhausted he continued to fight the fires with his bare hands. Despite horrific burns he managed to put the fires out and prevented them from restarting, which enabled the pilot to bring the almost totally wrecked bomber back safely. Sergeant Hannah never really recovered from his wounds although he survived to be awarded the first Victoria Cross to be won by a Scottish born airman for gallantry in the air. In addition to being the first Scot of the war to win the country's highest decoration for gallantry he was the youngest recipient of the medal in the Second World War.

The supremacy of the Royal Air Force continued throughout 1940 and into 1941. The Coastal Command were carrying out daily patrols in the search for enemy shipping. They were particularly interested in the German naval raiders the "Gneisenau" and the "Scharnhorst" which were known to be hiding in the port of Brest after a very successful operational patrol in the Atlantic. The ships had been photographed in Brest harbour and several attempts had been made to try and sink them. A raid on 4 April 1941 had left an unexploded bomb close to the "Gniesnau" and fearful of the damage which this would cause if it exploded the Germans moved the ship into a more open and less heavily defended part of the harbour. This was the best time to make a determined attack on the harbour. On the night of 5 April 1941, for the attack on the ship 6 Beaufort Bombers were briefed, 3 to attack with torpedoes. One of the torpedo- carrying Beauforts was piloted by Saltcoats born Flying Officer Kenneth Campbell (fig.19). However as a result of weather condition in the area of the airfield only one of the bomb carrying aircraft was able to take off and even then was unable to locate its target. At dawn on the 6 April as flying Officer Campbell reached the target area he assumed that the bomb carrying aircraft had cleared the way for his torpedo attack. As he approached his target at zero feet above the waves it became obvious to him that he would have to miss the harbour wall by a few feet in order to give his torpedo enough running time to explode. As he closed for the kill the anti-aircraft guns opened fire at him from all directions. This curtain of fire was impossible to avoid and the aircraft was torn apart by numerous hits from the enemy guns. After releasing his torpedo an engine was seen to burst into flames and Campbell's Beaufort plunged into Brest harbour and sank in 40 feet of water. The Germans recovered the bodies of Flying Officer Campbell and his crew from the wreckage lying at the bottom of the harbour and buried them with full military honours in Brest Cemetery. For his gallantry in pressing home his attack on such an important target Flying Officer Kenneth Campbell won Scotland's second Victoria Cross of the war and first of 2 to be won by Scots born pilots serving in Coastal Command.

In North Africa the Italian Army in Libya was starting to pose a threat to British supply routes through the Suez Canal, so much so that in spite of the need back home troops were sent out in December 1940 to reinforce the desert army. General Wavell had driven the Italian army from the very border of Egypt. The Germans felt obliged to come to the aid of their allies and sent troops under the command of General Erwin Rommel to North Africa. This injection of well trained and equipped troops sent the British reeling back across the Egyptian border. The British troops besieged in the fortified town of Torbruk were the only threat to the already long communication line of Rommel.

In November 1941 it was already apparent that Rommel was a formidable enemy and if he were no longer at the head of the Afrika Korps the task of winning the war in North Africa would be so much easier. On 13 November 1941 after all the necessary preplanning had been carried out by British agents working with friendly Arab groups behind the enemy lines the men from 11th (Scottish) Commando were landed from His Majesty's Submarines "Torbay", commanded by Lieutenant Commander Anthony C C Miers, a Scot who was to win the Victoria Cross 5 months later in Corfu harbour, and "Talisman", with a plan to kill Rommel at his desert headquarters at Beda Littoria in Libya. The group were led by Temporary Lieutenant Colonel Geoffrey Keyes (fig.20) who was the son of Admiral Lord Keyes who during the last year of the Great War had Masterminded the raid on the German Navy in the Belgian port of Zeebrugge and in 1941 had become the Director of Combined Operations.

When the commandos were finally all ashore they made their way to a safe cave where their clothes were dried out. On 15 November they set out towards Rommel's headquarters in the desert moving by night and resting by day. At almost midnight on 17 November the guard dogs at the base suddenly started to bark. As a result of the commotion an Italian officer came out of a building to investigate. He was immediately confronted by one of Keyes' officers Captain Robin Campbell who was able to convince the Italian by a display of arrogant German as to their origins. The Italian officer returned to his billet totally reassured. At the same time Lieutenant Colonel Keyes was leading his men around to the rear of the house. When he found that the back door was locked he decided to carry out the attack through the front door. The Lieutenant Colonel and his men moved to the front of the house where he boldly marched up to the door and knocked loudly on it. The German soldier who opened it to find himself looking into the barrel of a gun carried by a British Officer. The German immediately grabbed the barrel and shouted an alarm. Before he could say exactly what was happening he was shot by one of the attackers. With all the element of surprise gone Keyes ordered his commandos to get into and through the house as quickly as possible. Lieutenant Colonel Keyes accompanied by Captain Campbell burst into a room containing about a dozen men emptied a full magazine into them, retired and closed the door behind them. At this point Captain Campbell drew the firing pin from a hand grenade and covered by Keyes opened the door and lobbed in the bomb. However before the grenade exploded there was a burst of machine gun fire from within the room and the leader of the raid fell to the floor mortally wounded. As the grenade exploded the gallant Lieutenant Colonel Keyes was being dragged into the hallway by Captain Campbell. Having been shot through the heart he had died almost immediately. A few moments later after the fighting had died down the body of the valiant officer was carried from the house into the garden. After a search of the house had been made the brave Captain Campbell was wounded by a grenade thrown by one of his own men and had to be left with the body of Lieutenant Colonel Keyes. For his gallantry and leadership throughout the whole time of the raid Geoffrey Keyes who had been born in Aberdour in Fife was awarded a posthumous Victoria Cross which added to the Military Cross he had already been decorated with for gallantry in Syria earlier in the war.

Although by a twist of fate Rommel was away from his headquarters at Beda Littoria at the time of the raid was so impressed by the courage of the attackers that he ordered his chaplain to conduct the funeral service for Lieutenant Colonel Keyes.

While the raid on Rommel's house was taking place, quite independently, the British garrison encircled in the port of Tobruk were trying to break out to link up with the 7th Armoured Brigade which was engaged with Rommel's Afrika Korps at an escarpment outside the defensive parameter known as Sidi Rezegh. Convinced that a major offensive was about to take place by the suddenness of the attack from Tobruk, and this coupled by the fact that he was already heavily involved against the Desert Rats, from the direction Rommel sent in some of his battle hardened Panzer Divisions. As the battle was shaping up on 2 fronts the 7th Armoured Brigade was sent out to face the might of the Panzers, while Acting Brigadier John (Jock) Campbell with his support groups, which were more commonly known as "Jock Columns" were sent to engage in battle at Sidi Rezegh. The battle began on November 21 1941 and was initially a tank battle. Throughout the day, which was remarkable for the amount of dust put up in the heat of the battle, the fighting was most desperate. However by evening the Infantry had secured their objectives. With the capture of part of the Ridge they could concentrate on joining up with the attackers coming out from Tobruk. At Sidi Rezegh, the morning of 22 November started with a calm, certainly relative to the previous days fighting. Moves to capture the remainder of the ridge were met with stiff opposition and in the ensuing tank battles the British suffered heavy casualties which caused them to return to a position about 5 mile behind the furthest point of their advance of the previous day.

During the 2 days of the battle for Sidi Rezegh Acting Brigadier Campbell displayed courage of the highest order by making sure that his presence was seen by his men at any point where the fighting was known to be at its heaviest. Travelling in his open topped staff car or even on foot he encouraged his men throughout the day of 21 November. The next day when the battle was starting to reach a climax he was again in the hottest parts of the battle encouraging his men and even on 2 occasions took the place of gunners who had been wounded. Although he himself was wounded in the final phase of the battle he refused to be evacuated and remained to maintain the spirit of his men during the difficult withdrawal stage of the battle. For his inspiration during the 2 days of the battle of Sidi Rezegh the Acting Brigadier whose father had a drapers shop in Thurso the town of his birth was awarded the Victoria Cross. Just 3 weeks after the award was announced in the London Gazette this gallant Scots Officer who had escaped almost unscathed in one of the fiercest battles of the Desert Campaign was tragically killed in a motor car accident near Halfaya Pass in Libya on 5 March 1942.

The battle in North Africa to remove Rommel from his foothold on Egypt finally ended in January 1942 when the "Desert Fox" had been chased all the way back to the town of El Agheila, from where he had started on his drive into Egypt many months before.

It was now the turn of the 8th Army to be engaged in a campaign in the desert with supply lines stretched to their limit.

As the war entered its third year the conflict was truly on a world scale because of the Japanese attack on the American Fleet an Pearl Harbour in Hawaii, which resulted in the immediate entry into the war of the United States of America on the side of Britain and France. As the war in North Africa flowed back and forth along the Mediterranean coastal routes the Royal Navy and the Royal Air Force were endeavouring to ensure that vital supply lines to the Desert Army were maintained.

Important amongst these efforts was that of His Majesty's Submarine Service. This was reflected in the fact that Submariners won 3 Victoria Crosses in just 16 days in this theatre of the war. Of particular interest is the award to Commander Anthony Miers (fig.22) of His Majesty's Submarine "Torbay". Commander Miers had been in command of this Submarine since it had been built and had operated in the Mediterranean throughout 1941 and had already won 2 Distinguished Service Orders. By the early part of 1942 the patrols against enemy shipping had become fairly routine, except for the occasional operation into enemy waters to land commandos, such as the group who had raided Rommel's headquarters in Libya. On 3 March 1942 in the middle of another routine patrol Commander Miers contacted a large enemy convoy escorted by 3 Italian Destroyers. The distance was too great to be certain of doing damage so he decided to follow them in order to give himself time to catch up with the slow moving enemy. Following at a safe distance and checking through his periscope he suddenly realised that the enemy were about to enter a harbour which he decided must be Corfu.

After having followed them so far he felt it was a pity not to carry on. By maintaining the safe distance and observing the exact route taken by the enemy ships he was able to enter the harbour without running aground or hitting any defensive mines. Once in the harbour Miers knew that he was surrounded in all but one side, his escape.

As daylight was rapidly coming to an end the Commander took the decision to spend the night in the harbour and attack at dawn. He ordered that the engines be stopped and he settled down for a long wait on the sea bed. However in the middle of the night Commander Miers was given some disturbing news by his Engineer, the batteries would have to be recharged (an operation which required the Submarine to be on the surface). All the crew were briefed that no one was to talk unless it was absolutely necessary, and even then only in a whisper. When he surfaced it was almost like daylight in the eerie moonlight. The batteries were able to be recharged without incident and "Torbay" returned to the bottom of the harbour. When the morning came Commander Miers launched his attack. Travelling at Full Steam Ahead he went further into the harbour and as he was performing a full speed turn he ordered that the torpedoes be fired as the ships crossed his view in the periscope. Even before he had completed a 180 degree turn he heard 2 resounding explosions. After ordering a crash dive he and his ship returned to lie silently on the sea bed where they listened to the enemy scrambling about in a fruitless effort to locate the culprit. In a further 30 minutes he felt the time was right to make his dash to the open waters of the Mediterranean, and after out manoeuvreing the enemy anti-submarine patrols and depth charges he made the open waters after he had spend 17 hours in the enemy harbour.

On 28 July 1942 Commander Miers was presented with his Victoria Cross by His Majesty King George VI at a special ceremony in Buckingham Palace. At the same time the rest of the crew of His Majesty's Submarine "Torbay" joined their gallant Commander to receive their individual awards for their courage in Corfu harbour.

In spite of the efforts being made by the Senior and Junior Services in the Mediterranean the Army in North Africa found itself pushed back to within 60 miles of Alexandria. General Montgomery who had been appointed by Prime Minister Winston Churchill and ordered to destroy the Axis Forces commanded by Field Marshal Rommel was now in command of a Desert Army which was not prepared to retreat any further.

In late 1942 intelligence sources let it be known that Rommel was about to make a final attempt to force the 8th Army into the sea and march on Cairo. Having been forced back to a small town with a railway station that was to be on the lips of everyone back in Britain the 8th Army fought the first battle of Alamein at a place called Alam Halfa on the evening of 30 August 1942 when the Allied positions there were attacked by Rommel's Afrika Korps. Seven days later the Axis forces had withdrawn from the field of battle having lost more than 3,000 men and 50 tanks. This withdrawal gave Montgomery time to consolidate his forces and after a massive deployment of men and supplies was able to contemplate an advance against Rommel.

By early October General Montgomery's plan was ready and Allied bombers began a concentrated bombing campaign against the supply lines of the Afrika Korps into Libya and even to the Italian Mainland. At 9.40pm on 23 October 1942 nearly 900 guns opened up and thus began the battle which was described by Churchill as the "beginning of the end" of the campaign against Hitler's Germany. The intensity of the initial barrages of the Battle of El Alamein continued, in the infantry and tank phases of the battle over the next few days. By 4 November Rommel had received orders from Hitler himself to withdraw and by the end of that day the 8th Army had advanced 60 miles from Alamein. The Axis forces were in a full retreat which was to continue almost uninterrupted until the whole of the North Africa was in Allied hands.

As the bombing of Rommel's supply lines continued another Scot serving as a pilot in the 18th Squadron of the Royal Air Force distinguished himself. He was Wing Commander Hugh Malcolm (fig.23) from Broughty Ferry near Dundee. Wing Commander Malcolm displayed great skill and daring throughout his service in North Africa. Flying Bristol Blenheim bombers the pilots of the 18th Squadron were employed in attacking Rommel's airfields in an effort to destroy the Luftwaffe's response to the Royal Air Force's air supremacy. During November 1942 Wing Commander Malcolm led his men on 2 attacks on Bizerta airfield far behind the retreating Axis forces, both of which were successfully completed and all the aircraft returned safely. Again on 4 December he led his flight of 10 light bombers against an enemy airfield near Chougui. When they reached the target and were starting to move into the attack the flight was intercepted by a greater force of enemy fighters. One by one the bombers were shot down and through this Wing Commander Malcolm carried on with his attack until he himself like the other nine aircraft was shot down. His aircraft engulfed in a sheet of flame was seen to hit the ground and explode. For his leadership during the period from November until his death at Chougui on 4 December 1942 Wing Commander Malcolm was awarded the third Victoria Cross for a Scots born Airman.

As the war in North Africa moved into yet another year the Axis Army was being squeezed from both directions after the greatest seaborne invasion of the war to that date on 7 November when a joint American and British Force under the command of General Dwight D Eisenhower landed in Vichy occupied Morocco and Algiers. The 8th Army had advanced almost 800 miles across the desert of North Africa and by the end of January 1943 the men of the 51st (Highland) Division piped in by a Gordon Highlander entered Tripoli. The Desert Army had travelled an unbelievable total of 1,400 miles since that night of 23 October 1942.

The pincers were now closing, but Rommel and his Afrika Korps was not going to give up easily. After a brief period of rest after the capture of Tripoli the men of the 8th Army continued with the advance across Libya and into Tunisia. By March 1943 Rommel was a sick man, both in his own personal health and that of his Afrika Korps. On 6 March 1943 Rommel faced the might of the 8th Army for the last time at defensive positions known as the Mareth Line, where his forces held fast until his departure from Africa after which they were again forced into a retreat.

After the breakthrough at Mareth it became obvious that the next major fight would be for the town of Gabes which stood in the way of the advance towards General Eisenhower's forces. However the Afrika Korps decided to make its stand at Wadi Akarit, a feature which could be defended without much fear of an outflanking move by the British. The Battle of Wadi Akarit began on 5 April 1943 and once again the 8th Army was facing an Axis Army dug in well defended positions. As night fell the position had not changed as the enemy still were well dug in and the attackers were trying desperately to dislodge them. On the following day the men of the 7th Battalion of the Argyll and Sutherland Highlanders, part of the 51st (Highland) Division, which was one of 3 Divisions given the task of breaking out to capture the fortified hill of Jebel Roumana. The specific task allotted to the men of the 7th Argyll's was to attack and capture an anti-tank ditch along the enemy positions of the Wadi Akarit. The exploits of the Argyll's are embodied in the courage of the Commanding Officer of the Battalion Temporary Lieutenant Colonel Lorne Campbell (fig.24). Lieutenant Colonel Campbell in every sense of the word took control of the battlefield and inspired his men at all times during the 2 days of the battle, by his presence in the very forward parts cheering the men on and moving amongst them when the fighting was at its heaviest. There is not doubt that without the inspirational leadership of this Officer the bridgehead secured by his men would have quickly been lost to the enemy again. For his leadership during the attacks by and upon his Battalion The Argyll's Commanding Officer who was born in Argyllshire was decorated with the Victoria Cross.

After the Battle at Wadi Akarit the campaign in North Africa quickly came to an end and by May of 1943 the British 8th and Anglo American 1st Armies had met and were in control across the whole of North Africa. With Rommel defeated the way was clear for the Allies to strike at the soft under belly of Europe. In June 1943 the Allied army attacked and captured the island fortress of Pantellaria, which was only a short stepping stone from Sicily itself. The 8th Army landed shortly afterwards, in July, on Sicily and by the beginning of September the conquest was complete and the moves towards the Italian mainland commenced.

The Allies, now free to concentrate on the overthrow of Hitler, began to attack the Germans in their own, albeit stolen, territory. As with many wartime activities the Royal Navy played a vital role in maintaining supply lines which cut through waters controlled by the enemy from the Atlantic southern coast of France up to the Norwegian coast in the Arctic Circle. The role of the Royal Navy's Surface Ships and Submarines was to say the least, vital. In 1940 when Britain stood alone against the Germans the Navy in spite of not being able to use her larger ships, because of the air strength of the Luftwaffe, plays a great part in preventing a well planned invasion of Britain. At the same time when the German blockade of our coasts was at its most intensive and the U Boat Wolf Packs were roaming free in the North Atlantic, the Navy played its part in ensuring that vital food supplies were brought into Britain by the Merchant Navy.

By late 1943 the roles of hunter and hunted were reversed and Britain's Navy was now in the driving seat and looking for ways to strike at the heart of the German Navy.

Starting out on 11 September 1943 6 Midget Submarines, or X Craft as they were known set out for the northern anchorage of the German surface raiders "Lutzow", "Scharnhorst" and "Tirpitz" hidden in Kaafjord in northern Norway. These tiny craft were not able to travel the 1,000 miles of open sea without being towed by conventional submarines to within range of their targets which lay about 60 miles up the fjord. Before this fleet had reached the drop off point 3 of the X Craft had been lost. Of the 3 which were lost 2 disappeared completely and the third malfunctioned. The 3 midget submarines which had survived the journey across the ocean had all been targeted to the "Tirpitz" so it was decided that the attack would continue with the attack on "Tirpitz", the largest of the 3 ships and the biggest prize anyway, and forget about the other 2 ships. In the early morning of 20 September 1943, X5, X6 and X7 the 3 remaining X Craft slipped their tow ropes and headed for Norwegian waters. Although acting as a team the X Craft had no contact with each other as they made their way up the heavily defended approaches to the German warships. By 21 September they had manoeuvred their way through the minefield guarding the entrance to the fjord where the target lay. Travelling at periscope depth they made good time and were able to take avoiding action if any enemy ships appeared in their vision. As they reached the head of the fjord the most hazardous obstacle of the whole trip loomed up, the anti-submarine net. X6, commanded by Lieutenant Donald Cameron (fig.25), was able to get through when the net was opened to let through an enemy vessel. Once through he immediately dived in the deeper water inside the net. Meanwhile X7, commanded by Lieutenant Basil Place which had gone through the net earlier had been caught in the anti-torpedo net protecting the ships. By continuing to follow the ship which had allowed passage through the anti-submarine net Cameron was able to take his craft inside the inner defences the anti-torpedo net. In the calm waters of the upper reaches of the fjord X6 ran aground and in the efforts to refloat her she broke the surface of the water beside the "Tirpitz". A lookout on board spotted this and reported what he had seen and was dismissed as having seen a porpoise or something similar and nothing was done. Taking advantage of these vital minutes of inaction Cameron moved his craft even closer to the battleship. In moving closer the craft struck a sunken rock and bounced up to the surface yet again. This time he was not seen and was again able to take advantage of a few more precious minutes. Almost under the "Tirpitz" he again got tangled in an under water obstacle and in his efforts to break free broke the surface for a third time. This time he was spotted and became the target of small arms fire and grenades from the deck of the enemy ship. In view of this attention Cameron crash dived the craft and lay beneath the gull of the German ship. Knowing that he could not escape the submarine commander ordered that all secret document relating to the X Craft should be destroyed, he decided to scuttle X6. However before he did this he planted the charges below as he thought the forward gun turrets of the ship. Surfacing X6, set it to scuttle the crew calmly surrendered to a German patrol boat in the vicinity. Although aware that the charges had been set beneath the ship and unsure as to what would happen when they went off the 4 men of the crew with slight arrogance allowed themselves to be interrogated by the Germans. The Germans were getting nowhere with their questioning when X7 was sighted breaking the surface about 30 yards from the "Tirpitz". She immediately dived again and made for underneath the gull of the enemy ship and as she moved along the hull the charges were dropped, 1 under the forward turret and other about midships. In a vain attempt at escape X7 again became entangled in the anti-submarine netting.

At 12 minutes past 8 in the morning there was an explosion which ripped into the hull of the great ship. This caused a chain reaction and the charges set by X7 went off almost simultaneously. The

"Tirpitz" seemed to be lifted clear of the water and settled listing to port with a gaping hole in her hull. The 4 men from X6 were not hurt in the explosion but X7 was blown clear from the submerged object holding it fast. Unable to remain under water the midget submarine tried to make its escape on the surface. The commander managed to steer his craft alongside a moored ship and made his escape before it sank to the bottom. Another member of the crew bobbed to the surface 2 and a half hours later after trying in vain to rescue the other 2 who were trapped in the X Craft.

Nothing was ever heard again of the crew of X5 and the 6 surviving from X6 and X7 were all decorated for their gallantry including Carluke born Lieutenant Donald Cameron, along with Lieutenant Basil Godfrey Place, was awarded the last Victoria Cross to be awarded to a Scot serving in His Majesty's Royal Navy.

From the very start of the war it was apparent that the role of aircraft would be important in bringing it to a satisfactory conclusion. Hitler had tried to bring Britain to her knees by the use of massed bombing on non-military targets and by 1943 the Royal Air Force was using the same massed bomber technique on the cities of Germany. Bomber Command was by then concentrating on the destruction of the German war effort. The Royal Air Force was operating mainly at night while the American Air Force was in operation mainly in daytime with extensive fighter cover.

On 3 November 1943 Flight Lieutenant William Reid (fig.26) from Baillieston near Glasgow was one of the pilots of 61 Squadron, Royal Air Force Volunteer Reserve, flying Lancaster Bombers who set out that evening to bomb industrial targets around Dusseldorf in the Rhine Valley. Flying over Holland shortly after they had crossed the coast a Luftwaffe night fighter attacked from behind and because the rear gunner was unable to alert the rest of the crew, inflicted serious damage to the plane and more importantly to the pilot. The first that Flight Lieutenant Reid knew of the attack was when machine gun bullets shattered the perspex of the windscreen and wounded him in the head, shoulders and hand. Undeterred the Baillieston born pilot pressed on with his mission. A few miles further on another night fighter decided to have a go at the luckless aircraft. In spite of the attention from the air gunners in the Lancaster the German pilot was able to riddle the aircraft with cannon shells. This time killing the Navigator, fatally wounding the wireless operator and again wounding Reid and his flight Engineer. Realising that he and his bomber were in a serious situation the Flight Lieutenant decided once more to continue with the bombing mission. Once over his target he was able to successfully complete his bomb run and immediately start back for home. Several times on the way back to base the gallant pilot lost consciousness and with the help from the remaining members of the crew was able to crash land Lancaster "O" for Oboe on Shipdham airstrip (an American air force base in Norfolk). For his gallantry in continuing when many would have taken the chance to return home Flight Lieutenant William Reid was awarded a much deserved Victoria Cross.

Although by 1943 the submarine menace to British shipping had subsided there was still a need to keep the German "U" boats under control. Most of this work was carried out by the men of Coastal Command of the Royal Air Force. During the whole of the Second World War Coastal Command sank 189 enemy submarines, shared in the sinking of another 24 and damaged a further 385. The sinking of one of these submarines resulted in the award of the Victoria Cross to Aberdeen born John Cruickshank (fig.27).

Setting out from Sullom Voe in Shetland on the evening of 17 July 1944, Flying Officer John Cruickshank and his 9 man crew from 210 Squadron of the Royal Air Force Volunteer Reserve embarked on what started out as fairly uneventful anti-submarine patrol. After patrolling for 8 hours the Catalina's radar showed a faint signal which indicated an object about 40 miles away. About 20 minutes later a visual contact was made with a submarine travelling on the surface. In order to identify the submarine Cruickshank ordered that a certain code be flashed to it as it was known that British submarines were operating in the vicinity. Immediately the aircraft was met by a burst of fire from the submarine. Swinging round the pilot moved in at 50 feet above sea level and launched his attack on the enemy. With all guns firing he flew over the "U" boat to release the depth charges. As he pressed the release button nothing happened so the pilot took the aircraft out of the immediate danger to allow his crew to fix the problem with the mechanism. As Cruickshank commenced his second attempt at depth charging the fire from the submarine began to tear into the Catalina. One of the flak shells from the submarine burst inside the plane, wounding more of the crew including the pilot (the Bomb Aimer had been killed in the first attack). Undeterred by his wounds John Cruickshank continued with the attack and at the correct moment released 6 depth charges which perfectly straddled the submarine and sent it to the bottom. At this critical moment the pilot collapsed and the second pilot took over the controls. When Cruickshank awoke he refused medical help in case the morphine would impair his judgement. By this time the fires in the Catalina were all under control and Flying Officer Cruickshank was taken to the rear of the plane. On the long journey home he endeavoured to remain conscious, and was mindful for the safety of his crew. The aircraft reached the safety of Sullom Voe 5 and a half hours after the attack. Realising that great skill would be needed to land the Catalina safely Cruickshank insisted on returning to the cockpit in order that he could help the less experienced second pilot. Although by this time he himself was badly in need of medical attention he steadfastly refused to allow the aircraft to land until he was sure it could be done without further risk to his crew. Even after it had landed he made sure it was beached properly in order that it could be salvaged. Once the brave pilot was on dry land he collapsed from loss of blood from what proved to be 72 wounds in his body. He was given a transfusion of blood on the shore before he was transported to hospital. For his actions on the anti-submarine patrol Flying Officer Cruickshank was awarded the last Vectorial Cross to be awarded to an airman serving in coastal Command. Of the 4 Crosses won by men of Coastal Command the award to John Cruickshank was the only one which was not posthumous.

Into the last year of the war the Royal Air Force continued with its bombing raids into the heart of Hitler's Germany. Having realised that concentrated bombing alone was not going to bring Hitler to his knees the morale deflating effect of continuous bombing on a smaller scale became the norm.

On the first of January 1945 a force of 10 Lancaster Bombers from 9 Squadron of the Royal Air Force Volunteer Reserve set out from their base in England to bomb factories on the Dortmund-Ems Canal in the heart of industrial Germany. Flight Sergeant George Thompson (fig.28) who was born in Trinity Gask in Perthshire was the Wireless Operator in the bomber flown by Pilot Officer Denton.

After a quieter than normal flight to the target this small force encountered heavy flak over it. The concentrated fire scored 2 direct hits on the Lancaster in which Thompson was flying. Realising that the shells must have hit the bomber well back in the fuselage Sergeant Thompson decided to go to the rear and check on the gunners. As he moved along the burning aircraft he realised that both gunners were trapped by the flames. After crossing a large hole in the fuselage he reached the Mid Upper Gunner and found him ablaze. Dragging him clear he quickly was able to put out the flames in his comrades clothing and place him in a place of relative safety. In spite of the severe burns sustained in putting out the flames with his bare hand he continued along to the Rear Gunner who was wounded and trapped at his guns. Once he had made him comfortable he again went forward to his pilot to report that both gunners were too badly injured to bale out. The pilot then decided to fly the aircraft back to its base. The crippled bomber crash landed back in England. One of the gunners did not survive as did Thompson who died from his burns 3 weeks later. For managing to bring his crippled Lancaster back home Flying Officer Denton was awarded the Distinguished Flying Cross and Flight Sergeant Thompson was awarded a posthumous Victoria Cross for rescuing the gunners in the burning bomber.

At the same time as the Royal Air Force realised that the war would have to be won on the ground the men who had invaded Europe on 6 June 1944 were pushing towards Berlin itself. By February 1945 the Allied Armies were massing to cross the River Rhine the last great obstacle on the road to Berlin. Once into Germany the enemy were defending their fatherland and every inch was won with a high cost in blood.

On 1 March 1945 men of the 2nd Battalion of the King's Shropshire Light Infantry were pinned down by fire from a farm building near Kervenheim in the Rhineland. Amongst those pinned down by the enemy was Glasgow soldier Private James Stokes (fig.29), who when he realised that his Regiment could not advance as long as they were held up by the fire, rushed forward firing from the hip as he went and entered the building. Before anyone could follow him he emerged with 12 prisoners. During his dash he was wounded but refused to go to the rear to be attended to. Continuing the advance with the rest of his platoon he again attacked another defended house and this time brought out 5 more prisoners. In this attack he was again wounded only this time more seriously and again he insisted in remaining with his platoon in the advance. As the men of the Shropshire Light Infantry reached their objective Private Stokes was mortally wounded as he charged for the third time and fell only 20 yards from the enemy position. For his actions on this day the soldier who before the war was a storeman in a large Glasgow warehouse was awarded the last Victoria Cross to be won by a Scot, but unfortunately he had died in winning it.

Although the war with Germany ended soon after the death of Jimmy Stokes the war with Japan continued until the Atomic Bombs were dropped on Hiroshima and Nagasaki in August 1945. No further awards of the Victoria Cross were made to Scots born servicemen although 8 more awards were won after the fall of Germany and before the fall of Japan.

During the Second World War a total of 183 Crosses were won by 182 soldiers, sailors and airmen and 12 of these were awarded to Scots.

CHAPTER 4

SOME CAMEOS

On a cold Sunday November morning in 1971 at Horse Guards Parade in London a young Corporal in the Royal Military Police was in charge of arranging the many hundreds of members of the Royal British Legion in preparation for the march past the Cenotaph in Whitehall at the end of the Armistice ceremony. Many of the bemedalled ex-servicemen wished to march in the front rank. Suddenly someone tapped the Corporal on the shoulder and said "Corporal, I think this man should be in the front rank" and he pushed forward a little old man wearing an equally old grey coat looking a mixture of yellow with old age and blue with the cold. This old ex-serviceman was no different from the many hundreds around him except that attached to the long coat was the ribbon of the Victoria Cross and three Great War medals.

The Military Policeman never found out the old man's name but there is no doubt that he is long since dead and definitely still as anonymous.

In Scotland today the names and stories of those winners born there are equally unknown and in the following pages I hope to recount the life stories as far as is possible of a few of these heroes. As will be seen they come from varying backgrounds and are almost completely unknown in the towns of their birth.

PRIVATE RODERICK MCGREGOR

1st BATTALION THE RIFLE BRIGADE (PRINCE CONSORT'S OWN)

Roderick McGregor was born in the early 1820's (probably 1822 although some sources give his year of birth as 1824) in the Dunain district of Inverness-shire. Much of early life was concerned with working on the land which lasted until his twentieth year when young Roderick sought out more adventure in his life. In June 1842 he left his native Inverness-shire, destined not to return for more than 20 years and enlisted in the 1st Battalion of the Rifle Brigade. After the completion of his basic training in early 1843 Number 2074 Private McGregor was posted to the 2nd Battalion of his chosen regiment. Shortly after his arrival at the Battalion it was moved across the Atlantic Ocean and remained in Canada until 1852. In that year the regiment was recalled from overseas and arrived back in England in time to take a leading role in the funeral procession of the Colonel-in-Chief of the Rifle Brigade, the Duke of Wellington, as he was laid to rest in St. Paul's Cathedral.

As the crisis in the Crimea began to develop the 1st and 2nd Battalions of the Rifle Brigade again moved overseas and landed in the Balkans in preparation for the expected war with Russia. In September 1854 both Battalions took part in the unopposed landings in the Crimea. On the 19 September 1854 the men of the Rifle Brigade including Roderick McGregor had their first taste of real action when they engaged a Russian force across the River Bulganak. The unprepared force of the enemy were quickly driven back and the following day the men of the 2nd Battalion led the advance across the next line of Russian defence at the River Alma. During this early period of the war the advance of the British Army seemed unstoppable and the enemy were quickly retreating towards Sebastopol.

After the opening action the men of the Rifle Brigade were not employed except for a few who had taken part in the Battle of Balaclava in 26 October 1854 until the action at Inkerman on the 5 November of that year. Roderick McGregor was one of the Battalion present at the Battle of Inkerman.

When the privation of the first winter of the war began to take its toll, the men of the Rifle Brigade settled in as best they could to the task of besieging the Russian Army within Sebastopol. It was during this prolonged siege that Private McGregor displayed the courage which resulted in him being awarded the Victoria Cross.

He was one of the 62 men who had survived to receive their decorations from Her Majesty Queen Victoria at a very special ceremony in Hyde Park in London on 26 June 1857. The Queen herself pinned to his breast alongside the Crimea Campaign Medal with the clasps which denoted that he had taken part in the battles at the Alma, Inkerman and the siege of Sebastopol.

After the end of the war with Russia the men of the Rifle Brigade returned to Britain and for a short time served in Ireland. Before long news was received of the unrest in India and the now promoted Corporal McGregor sailed from Dublin into action once more. In India his regiment was part of the force which finally captured the city of Lucknow in March 1858. He survived the Indian Mutiny unscathed and received the medal issued to all who had taken part in it.

After 5 years more service Roderick McGregor with a total of 21 years under the Colours, 4 medals including the Victoria Cross and a valuable pension of £10 per year for life left the army. After his discharge from the army he came home to Inverness-shire and married Miss Isobella MacDonald. The local landlord knowing of his military exploits made available to him and his new wife a piece of ground at a nominal rent on which to build a house. This piece of ground on the Bunloit Estate near Drumnadrochit was developed into a croft and is to this day still known as "The Pensioners Croft". Apart from his crofting interests he also acted as the School Board Officer for the Bunloit part of the parish.

His time in the trenches during that first winter of the war in the Crimea had taken its toll of his health and he began to suffer and was for a long time the victim of Bronchitis. During his years in retirement he was often visited by officers of his old regiment who when in the area were always keen to visit one of the heroes of the Rifle Brigade.

On 9 August 1888 in his 66th year, the illness which had been with him for many years finally laid him to rest and he was buried in his local cemetery at Drumnadrochit. When his regiment became aware of his death later on in that year a subscription was made for a memorial to this crofter who was of such a high standing in the annals of one of the country's oldest regiments. Today that memorial is maintained in such a condition that one could be forgiven for thinking that it had only recently been erected instead of nearly a century ago.

LIEUTENANT COLONEL JOHN C. MCNEILL

107th FOOT

John McNeill became the Laird of Colonsay, the place of his birth, more than a quarter of a century after he could have rightly expected to hold that title. His father Captain Alexander McNeill, who had been the eldest son of Lord Colonsay, was drowned in an accident when John was still in his teens. On the death of Lord Colonsay the title went to the next surviving son also called John. In 1877 his Uncle offered Colonsay to Sir John at the highly inflated price of £80,000. In that year he regained the title which, had his father survived, he would have had by right of succession. When he returned to his island Sir John had already become one of the most decorated and famous of Queen Victoria's soldiers.

John Carstairs McNeill born on 28 March 1831 was destined to follow a military career. After his early education at St. Andrew's he went on to further his education at Addiscombe in preparation for his entry into the Indian Army. From Addiscombe he was gazetted into the 12th Bengal Native Infantry, a regiment which mutinied at Jhansi in June 1857. Having lost his regiment he spent the rest of the campaign as Aide-de-camp to General Sir Edward Lugard. After the mutiny had been quashed new regiments were formed and it was in 1861 that he was gazette to, but never actually joined, the 107th regiment of Foot. Instead he transferred to the 48th Foot. On 30 March 1864 while serving in New Zealand he was awarded the Victoria Cross for extreme gallantry, whilst still a Major, in rescuing from a band of about 50 natives a Private soldier who had been accompanying him.

On his return from New Zealand he commanded the Tipperary Flying Column during disturbances in Ireland in 1866 and 1867. After his valuable work in Ireland for which he was Mentioned in Despatches, he was sent to Canada as Military Secretary to Lord Lisgard, the Governor General. It was at this time that he met Lord Strathcona who was eventually to lend him the money to buy back his birthright.

From the relatively inactive military life in Canada he again returned to action when he was appointed 2nd in command of the expedition to Ashanti in 1873. During this time he was severely wounded and again Mentioned in Despatches. After recovering from his wounds he was appointed Equerry to Her Majesty Queen Victoria, a post he held until he was again called to serve his country in the war in Egypt in 1882. With the rank of Major General he served with distinction throughout and was almost killed during an attack on his fortifications in the desert near Suakim on 22 March 1885. When the alarm had been given of the enemy's attack Sir John was outside the defences on his horse. As he attempted to spur his horse the animal rose up and deposited the General on the sand as a band of natives closed in on him. In an action not dissimilar to the one that had won him the Victoria Cross his Aide-de-Camp galloped to his rescue and saved his life.

After the war in Egypt had ended he once more returned to the Island of Colonsay where he became involved in a struggle of a different sort. Some bad business investments had resulted in financial difficulties which he had tried to offset by increasing the rents for the tenants of the crofts in Colonsay. Although he had taken time to learn Gaelic, the language of his tenants, they had little respect for him when according to an article in The Oban Times, the rents had increased by amounts ranging from about 50% to 100%. This massive increase resulted in arrears and according to the records of the Crofters Commission in 1889, he sued his tenants for unpaid rent saying "Otherwise sequestration for the farmers and eviction for the crofters". Eventually his claim was ruled out of court as incompetent and he finally gave up his claim in 1892.

When King Edward VII came to the throne Sir John was again appointed Equerry to the monarch. The new King even visited him in Colonsay shortly after his coronation in 1902.

On 25 May 1904, Sir John Carstairs McNeill V.C.,G.C.V.O.,K.C.B.,K.C.M.G., died in London and his body was taken home to Colonsay where he was interred in the McNeill Chapel in Oronsay Priory.

As Sir John had died unmarried and without an heir, Colonsay was taken over by Lord Strathcona for the cost of the debt still owed by Sir John's estate.

SERGEANT DONALD D FARMER

QUEEN'S OWN CAMERON HIGHLANDERS

In 1991 the Regimental Museum of the Queen's Own Highlanders received the medals including the Victoria Cross of Lieutenant Colonel Donald Dickson Farmer to complete the collection of Crosses awarded to men of the 79th Regiment.

Donald Farmer who was born on the 28th May 1877 joined the 1st Battalion of the Cameron Highlanders from his home in Kelso at the age of 14 years and 10 months. After his early training he served with the Battalion mainly in the Mediterranean at Malta. In late 1897 they were moved to Cairo where they were stationed in anticipation of being part of the Expeditionary Force which would be sent to recover the parts of Sudan which had been lost from Egypt's control when General Gordon was murdered at Khartoum in 1884. In January 1898 the 1st Battalion of the Queen's Own Cameron Highlanders, including Donald Farmer left Cairo and advanced across the desert to join the army in the Sudan. During the campaign he saw action at the battles of The Atbara and Khartoum.

After they returned from the Sudan young Donald was attached to the Mounted Infantry Company of the Battalion which had been formed in preparation for a move to the war in South Africa. The Battalion including Donald Farmer arrived in South Africa in March 1900. The men of the Camerons formed part of the Highland Brigade which took prominent parts in the actions against the Boer positions at Diamond Hill and Wittebergen in the summer of 1900. After these actions the Battalion remained in the area of the Orange River for the rest of the year and it was at Nooitgedacht on the 13th

December that the now Sergeant Farmer rescued his officer who had been wounded and carried him to safety before returning to the fight where he was eventually captured. As the Boers at this time were very mobile and did not wish the inconvenience of having to herd prisoners he was released after a few days and made his way back to the British lines where he was re-equipped and returned to his regiment

Sergeant Farmer was present at the parade in Pietermaritzburg on the 15th August 1901 when he and 49 others were presented by the Duke of York with awards for gallantry won during the war. In addition to his Victoria Cross he was also twice Mentioned in Despatches. When the Boers finally gave up the fight the Battalion returned to Fort George in Inverness in 1902 where the first Victoria Cross winner of the Queen's Own Cameron Highlanders captained the regimental football team.

On the 22nd February 1905 whilst serving in Ireland he was promoted to the rank of Colour Sergeant. In 1909 after his service in Ireland he was posted to one of the new Territorial Army battalions, the Liverpool Scottish as a Regular Army Instructor. While he was stationed in Liverpool he completed his twenty one year engagement. The following year in 1914 as the Regimental Sergeant Major of the 1st Battalion of the Liverpool Scottish he returned to action in France. In June 1915 after having been commissioned he joined the 2nd Battalion of the Liverpool Scottish and served with them up to the cessation of hostilities. After a long and distinguished military career in which he had served from the rank of Private he finally retired in 1921 as a Lieutenant Colonel.

Up to his death on the 23rd December 1956 Lieutenant Colonel Farmer played an active role in the running of the Liverpool Scottish Regimental Association, in which he had been a founder member.

SERGEANT JOHN MEIKLE

4th BATTALION THE SEAFORTH HIGHLANDERS

In the station square in Dingwall in Ross and Cromarty is a memorial to the only member of the 4th Seaforths to win the Victoria Cross in the Great War. This large slab of granite bears the inscription: "'In memory of Sergeant John Meikle V.C.,M.M., late clerk at Nitshill Station who enlisted in H M Forces (Seaforth Highlanders) 8th February 1915, during the Great War and was killed in action on 20th July 1918 ' Erected by his railway comrades."

John Meikle was the fifth of twelve children and was born at Kirkintilloch near Glasgow on the 11th September 1898. When he was 3 years old his family moved to Nitshill where his father was working. When he started school he attended Levern Primary School (which still remembers the deeds of its former pupil and indeed has a representation of the Victoria Cross embodied in the school badge.) When he left school he soon secured employment as a clerk at the local station of the Glasgow, Barrhead and Kilmarnock Railway Company. At the outbreak of the Great War he made many attempts to join up and was finally successful on the 8th February 1915 at the age of 16 years and 5 months. After he had been accepted within a month he had reported to Maryhill Barracks in Glasgow and enlisted in the 4th Battalion the Seaforth Highlanders (Territorial Force). When he had completed his initial training he decided to train in the use of the Lewis Gun. He soon became competent in his new weapon and eager to try out his new skills. Eager as he was it was several months before his Battalion went to France. John was quickly promoted and by the time of the battle of Passchendaele in the autumn of 1917 he had already been promoted to the rank of Corporal. After the battle he was allowed home on leave and he returned to Nitshill with a bayonet wound and a much deserved Military Medal.

After his brief flirtation with hero worship he again returned to the trenches in France and was soon promoted to Sergeant in recognition of his qualities of leadership. By the summer of 1918 the Germans had launched what was to be their last major effort to defeat the Allied Armies along the River Marne. The 51st Highland Division, including the 4th Seaforths, were dug in near the village of Marfaux. On the 20th July men of Sergeant Meikle's company were being mowed down each time they came across an enemy machine gun nest. Twice during the day after his company had been held up in their advance by enemy machine gunners he attacked the nest and allowed his men to advance. Unfortunately as he led his men onto the enemy position for the second time he was killed at the moment of his success.

At the time of his death John Meikle had been in the army for only three and a half years, reached the rank of Sergeant and won 2 of the Country's highest awards for gallantry. His award of the Victoria Cross was gazetted exactly one week after what would have been his eighteenth birthday. His body was buried in the British War Cemetery at Marfaux in France and grateful workmates in the railway erected a memorial in January 1920 at Nitshill Station. This is the same stone which now stands in the Station Square in Dingwall, the home town of the 4th Battalion of the Seaforth Highlanders, to where it was removed in 1971 to protect it from the attention of vandals.

TEMPORARY CAPTAIN JOHN MACGREGOR

2nd C.M.R. 1st CENTRAL ONTARIO REGIMENT

John McGregor was born in Cawdor near Nairn on 1st February 1889. After attending Cawdor school he joined a local firm of builders and served his time as an apprentice to become a stonemason. On reaching the age of twenty he decided to seek his fortune on the other side of the Atlantic in Canada. After he had been in Canada for more than five years the European War broke out he decided that he wanted to fight for his country. In an effort to be one of the first Canadians to volunteer to fight in Europe he walked in snow shoes for over 120 miles to enlist in the Canadian Mounted Rifles. On reaching Vancouver in March 1915 he started his training and by the 22nd September of that year he was in the trenches of France, where he quickly gained promotions to the rank of Sergeant.

When the Canadian Infantry launched their now famous attack on the Germans defending Vimy Ridge in April 1917 it was Sergeant John MacGregor who led the charge which resulted in him being the first of the Canadians to reach the summit of the ridge. For this act of conspicuous gallantry he was decorated with the Distinguished Conduct Medal and immediately given a commission in the field. As Lieutenant MacGregor he was also Mentioned in Despatches in January 1918 for leading a trench raid deep onto the enemy held position known as Hill 70. Later the same month he was awarded the first of his Military Crosses and further promoted to the rank of Captain. Before the year was finished he was decorated twice more with a second Military Cross and the Country's highest decoration for gallantry, the Victoria Cross. This was awarded for the most conspicuous bravery during the period 29th September to 3rd October 1918 at the height of the fighting at Cambrai. His action at this time earned him the title of "Fighting Mac of the Canadian Mounted Rifles" in recognition of his outstanding leadership and self sacrifice.

With the war now over the newly promoted Major MacGregor was able to visit his family and friends in Cawdor where he was showered with gifts from a grateful public who appreciated what this famous son of Cawdor had achieved. Later that year he left the army as a Major and returned to his real profession as a stonemason.

In 1929 he again returned to Britain for the dual purpose of attending the special banquet which had been organised in order that the Prince of Wales could meet the surviving holders of the Victoria Cross and more importantly as far as he was concerned he could visit his eighty year old mother who still lived in the family home in Cawdor. After his visit was over he again returned to his new home in British Columbia.

In 1939 the drums of war were heard in Europe and again he joined to fight the cause of the land of his birth and he managed in spite of his age to get himself posted back to Britain. Although he served in England until the end of the war he still managed in 1943 to bring his son who was serving in the Royal Canadian Air Force to meet the people of his place of birth.

After yet another war away from Canada he returned to his new homeland where he remained until after a long illness he died on the 9th June 1952 in the hospital at Powell River in British Columbia.

COMMANDER ANTHONY C.C. MIERS

ROYAL NAVY

Tony Miers was a character. There are many stories about him, most of them are true. This is how Vice "Admiral Sir Roderick MacDonald described his long time friend and colleague.

On 28 July 1942 at Buckingham Palace His Majesty King George VI decorated the Captain and crew of HM Submarine "Torbay". An occasion unique in that it was the first time that both officers and men of one of HM's ships had appeared at the same investiture to receive decorations. It was as the result of direct intervention on the part of the submarine's Commander Tony Miers who let it be known that if his crew were not to be with him when he was to receive his Victoria Cross then he did not wish to receive it. As a result of this for the first time the whole crew were together at the time when their Captain was to be honoured. On that day the 27 members of that submarine received decorations for gallantry.

It was inevitable that Tony Miers would be decorated for bravery, as gallantry was and still is something of a family tradition. Before the Great War his father received a Lifesaving Medal, his elder brother, Colonel Ronald Capel Miers, received a Distinguished Service Order whilst serving in the "family" regiment, The Queen's Own Cameron Highlanders, during the 1939/45 war and his son, John, serving in the Submarines received the Queen's Commendation for Brave Conduct for courage and leadership during rescue and salvage operations when 2 ships collided off Gibraltar in June 1978.

Anthony Cecil Capel Miers was born at Birchwood, Inverness on 11 November 1906. He was the younger son of Captain Douglas Miers of the Queen's Own Cameron Highlanders who died in action in France on the 25 September 1914 (a date which was to have some superstition throughout the life of Admiral Miers). His early education was at Edinburgh Academy and a preparatory school Stubbington House. He eventually went on to Wellington College. As a result of poor eyesight he failed the medical that would allow him to take the then traditional route to the Royal Navy via Dartmouth. He did however enter later by the examination known as Special Entry after his eyesight had improved significantly.

He joined the Royal Navy as a cadet in 1924 and after service as a Midshipman in HMS "Valiant" and other ships he transferred to submarines in 1929. His wife said he used to enjoy telling people that he was "conscripted" into the Submarine service. He was promoted to the rank of Lieutenant in 1930 and commanded his first submarine the E Class E54 during 1936/37. The following year as Lieutenant Commander he served on the staff of the Admiral of the Fleet, Sir Charles Forbes. When he had finished his employment with the Home Fleet he returned to his beloved submarines already having been Mentioned in Despatches.

In the summer of 1940 he took command of HMS Torbay and by the time he left her in 1943 in addition to having been promoted Commander he had also been decorated with the Victoria Cross, for the action on 4 March 1942 in Corfu Harbour when he took his submarine into the very jaws of the enemy and returned after having removed more than a few teeth. He was also awarded two Distinguished Service Orders for his part in sinking at least 11 enemy ships during his numerous patrols in the waters of the Mediterranean.

Subsequently he was appointed to the staff of Admiral Chester Nimitz as the British Liaison Officer in the American Pacific Fleet. After his flirtation with the American Navy he returned in 1944 to his first love and took command of the 8th Submarine Flotilla.

"Lucky in war, lucky in love" was a favourite expression of Tony Miers and in 1945 after what he considered a very lucky war he married Patricia Mary Millar, a Scottish Bankers daughter to bring his belief into fruition.

After the war he was promoted to Captain and in anticipation of taking over the Royal Naval Air Station, HMS "Blackcap" at the age of 42 he gained his pilots licence. The early 1950's saw him again in command of submarines, this time the 1st Submarine Flotilla in the Mediterranean. A shore job took him to the Royal Naval College at Greenwich from which he was appointed to the rank of Rear Admiral and became the Flag Officer Middle East, where he returned to the scene of some of his greatest exploits in time to help combat the threat from E.O.K.A. terrorists in Cyprus.

Admiral Miers retired from the Navy early in 1959 and was surprised to read in The Times that he had been Knighted in the June 1959 Birthday Honours, this was considered unusual as he was a Rear Admiral and Knighthoods traditionally went to Vice Admirals and above. He often returned to his native Inverness, where he is buried. He died on 30 June 1985.

Amongst the many honours bestowed upon Tony Miers was the Freedom of the City of London and more especially in 1955 he received the freedom of the town of his birth the Royal Burgh of Inverness.

FLIGHT LIEUTENANT WILLIAM REID

61 SQUADRON ROYAL AIR FORCE VOLUNTEER RESERVE

In May 1944 a young man, who just over three years previously had left school to join the Royal Air Force, stood before the assembled pupils of Coatbridge Academy, some of whom had remembered the former pupil, to receive the accolade befitting a winner of Britain's highest award for gallantry in the face of an enemy. At the same time he was presented with a silver cup inscribed with the citation for his Victoria Cross, and a cheque for £1000 from the people of Baillieston. This was presented by the oldest resident who was in fact a relative of his own.

William Reid was born on 21 December 1921 at No.43 Main Street, Baillieston near Glasgow. He was one of five children, whose parents ran a small shop next to the house he was born in, and attended the local school in Baillieston up to the age of eleven years. In 1932 he went to the nearest secondary school to his home, Coatbridge Academy.

When war broke out he wanted to join up, however, he had to finish his education. After leaving school and going to night school for three months, he volunteered for the Royal Air Force as he already had his brother George serving as a Wireless Operator/Air Gunner in Blenheims. At that time so many young men were wanting to join up as pilots that there was a waiting list, so young Bill Reid was put on the Volunteer Reserve. His brother was reported missing presumed killed in a raid over Belgium. He had various jobs, including Christmas relief postman before he finally secured employment with a Government agency, the Scottish Land Group. In August 1941, a week after his father died, he was working in a quarry when word reached him that he had been called up to join the Royal Air Force as Aircrew.

After he had reported to the Aircrew Reception Centre in London he was sent to No.8 Squadron at Newquay. After completing his early training he moved from the Initial Training Wing to Winslow, from where he went to Avonmouth to board a ship which took him to New Brunswick in Canada. Once in Canada he moved south to California travelling in civilian clothes as America had not yet entered the war, where the weather for flying could be guaranteed.

After seven months and over 200 hours flying he gained his Pilots Wings and returned to Little Rissington in Gloucestershire where he graduated onto the two engined Airspeed Oxford Advanced Trainer. After mastering the Oxford he was sent to No.29 Operational Training Unit at North Luffenham in Rutland to continue his training in Wellington Bombers. Whilst he was there he was asked to pick the crew which would train with him. His progress had been so outstanding that he was asked to remain there as an Instructor. Initially he refused this offer, but after he was guaranteed a Lancaster posting he agreed to stay on for a further six months. When he was still at 29 O.T.U. his crew went in different aircraft on a raid on Munchen Gladbach and it was on this that his original choice of navigator for his own crew was lost in action. It was then that Allan Jeffries from Perth in Western Australia joined his crew.

At the end of September 1943 he was posted to No. 61 Squadron to fly Lancaster Bombers. His first nine trips into enemy territory were in his own words "fairly uneventful, just searchlights to annoy". His log book shows that he was diverted six times and on two occasions nearly came to grief when he almost collided with other aircraft.

However on his tenth flight, on 3 November 1943, a raid on the Mannesman Steelworks in Dusseldorf Flight Lieutenant Reid showed such devotion to duty when he carried on with his mission even after he had been severely wounded on the outward journey. Many would have turned back but he continued saying nothing of his wounds. The plane was attacked once again and this time his Navigator Allan Jeffries was killed and his Wireless Operator Jim Mann was fatally wounded. After completing his bomb run, he set a course for home and managed to land the badly damaged Lancaster safely at Shipdham an American Air base in Norfolk. The American doctors patched him up before sending him to hospital in Norwich. Three days later he was sent to Ely hospital where he remained for five weeks.

At the end of the first week of December 1943 photographers started to arrive and take his photograph. Aware that his Flight Engineer Jim Norris had been awarded the Conspicuous Gallantry Medal he suspected that he as Pilot had been awarded the Distinguished Service Order. However when Air Vice Marshal Ralph Cochrane phoned on the 13 December to congratulate him on the award of the Victoria Cross he almost fainted. When he had fully recovered from his wounds he was given a months sick leave, during which time he was invited to visit the A.V. Roe Factory where his plane was built. There he received a silver model of a Lancaster Bomber. Shortly before his leave was due to end he received another phone call from Air Vice Marshal Cochrane telling him that he wanted him to join 617 Squadron, the Dambusters. He was presented with his Victoria Cross at Buckingham Palace in June 1944 by His Majesty King George VI at an investiture attended by only those receiving decorations. As this was the time of great "Doodlebug" activity it was felt that it was too dangerous to invite guests to the Palace which was a recognised target.

After 24 more trips over enemy territory his luck finally ran out on 31 July 1944 when he was shot down during a raid on a bomb storage dump in a railway tunnel near Rhiems. As the aircraft plunged earthwards Bill Reid managed to escape, but unfortunately three of his crew died unable to get free from the doomed Lancaster. After he was interrogated he was sent to Dulag Luft 3B at Sagan in Poland. In early 1945 as the Russian Army advanced into Poland he was moved to a camp at Luckenwalde to the south of Berlin. In the depths of a European winter it was a very miserable time in his life and finally the camp was captured by the advancing Russians. Even then it was not over for he had to stagnate for almost a month before he and the other prisoners were handed over to the Americans at the River Elbe. From there he was flown in a Lancaster to Brussels and then to the Royal Air Force base at Lyneham. After a few days medical examination and debriefing he was given three months leave. He was demobbed from the service in November 1945.

While he was in the prison camp he had decided to leave the Royal Air Force and taking advantage of their sponsorship started at Glasgow University, while still in the service. After completing his course at Glasgow University and the West of Scotland College of Agriculture he graduated in 1949 with a B.Sc. in Agriculture. At University he had won a Lady MacRobert Scholarship and started work for the MacRobert Farms. He work for them for 10 years before moving on to employment with Spillers Limited. After 20 years with this firm he retired in 1980 and went to live in Crieff, where he still lives with his wife Violet whom he married in 1952.

When he is not involved with the Air Crew Association he spends his time gardening, playing golf and a bit of shooting. In 1968 he went with nine other winners of the Victoria Cross, including Tony Miers and Harold Wooley to Kenya as the guest of Kenya Airways who had just taken delivery of ten VC 10's each bearing the name of one of the guests.

There is in Coatbridge Academy an award which is still competed for annually the "William Reid VC Prize". His most recent accolade came on 12 May 1988 when he received the Freedom of the City of London in recognition of his service during the war and in particular for having won the highest award that this nation can bestow on anybody for bravery against an enemy, the Victoria Cross.

FLYING OFFICER JOHN A CRUICKSHANK

210 SQUADRON ROYAL AIR FORCE VOLUNTEER RESERVE

On the 21 September 1944 His Majesty King George VI presented to Flying Officer John A Cruickshank at an investiture at the Palace of Holyrood House, Edinburgh the Victoria Cross award for action against a German U-Boat during the evening of 17 July that year.

John Alexander Cruickshank was born in Aberdeen on 20 May 1920. He attended Aberdeen Grammar School initially and Daniel Stewart's College in Edinburgh. After finishing his schooling he joined the former Commercial Bank of Scotland in 1938. Like many young men in pre war Britain John Cruickshank had joined the Territorial Army in the 129th Field Regiment of the Royal Artillery. When war broke out he was called up and in 1941 volunteered to transfer to the Royal Air Force for air crew duties. Like many others at the time he had to move across the Atlantic to do his pilot training with the United States Navy at their base at Pensacola, Florida. A year later in July 1942 he received his pilots wings and returned home being posted to 210 Squadron, Coastal Command.

His Squadron was involved in day and night Anti U-Boat patrols in the Bay of Biscay and convoy escort duties in the south west approaches to the United Kingdom and in early 1944 in northern waters. On 17 July while on Anti U-Boat patrol in support of the Royal Navy Home Fleet engaged in a foray to northern Norway to destroy the German Battleship "Tirpitz", his aircraft sighted and attacked a German U-Boat threatening the safety of the Fleet. During his attack his aircraft was badly damaged by anti aircraft fire and Flying Officer John Dickson, the Navigator and Bomb Aimer was killed.

Cruickshank and other members of his crew were wounded but he pressed home his attack at 50 feet with the result the U-Boat was destroyed with the loss of all hands. Cruickshank and his crew were able to fly the damaged aircraft back to base in the Shetland Islands.

He was decorated with the Victoria Cross for his gallantry in this action. He was demobilised from the service in 1946 and resumed his banking career retiring in 1977. Today he is an Honorary Life Vice President of the Aircrew Association, a fitting honour to Scotlands only surviving Coastal Command Victoria Cross winner.

There are many stories to be told to remind us of Scotlands Forgotten Valour and time is rapidly running out before there are none left who could claim to be part of Scotland heroic past and still be remembered with the Wallace's and Bruce's of our history.

CHAPTER 5

MEMORABILIA

Apart from the actual medal memorabilia which celebrate the individual accomplishments of Victoria Cross winners come in many forms and in theory there is no winner who should not be remembered in some way or other. Unfortunately this is not the case as in spite of the human animal having the best developed brain in nature the memory section is probably one of the shortest in nature.

Individual winners are recorded on War Memorials usually in the place of their birth or where they were living prior to their death. Their names can also be seen in memorials dedicated to a particular Regimental or Service and occasionally plaques are attached to some prominent building or feature in a place which held some importance to the winners of the Victoria Cross in their lifetime. Although many died winning their medals, many survived the battlefields to die later and their exploits are commemorated on their gravestones.

Many regiments have pride of place for paintings depicting the actions in which some of their Victoria Crosses were won. The London Illustrated News published a supplement on 20 June 1857 as part of the very first announcement of winners of the Victoria Cross which showed in line drawing form the actions of some of the men who had won the Cross during the Crimean War.

Their actions are further commemorated by having their name given to various forms of transport including aircraft and trains, street names, seats, Regimental tunes as well as their exploits being immortalised in story and poetry.

It is over one hundred and thirty years since the award was instituted and in that time thirteen hundred and fifty men have been decorated with the award. Today there are very few of these men who are remembered and of these none are Scots. When the first announcements were made in 1856 there began a fascination amongst Victorians with the Victoria Cross, a fascination which remains today in a small band of enthusiasts for the winners of the medal.

When the Crimean War ended there had been a great interest in the conduct of the war because of the daily reports from the front by William Russell of the Times Newspaper. As well as creating the Victoria Cross and war correspondents the Crimean War gave for the first time memorials to these soldiers and sailors who had fallen in battle, previously only officers and gentlemen who had fallen merited a memorial. The national interest in the war changed all that and for the first time the names of those fallen heroes, including some who had won the Victoria Cross appeared on this new type of memorial. These memorials have for the most part been so eroded and weathered that the names of most have become so illegible that they are now lost in the mists of time.

The Victorians treated their heroes with respect and always had some in their midst because from its institution to the death of Queen Victoria all recipients had to survive to win the decoration, although a few were destined to die in some further act of gallantry a few days or even years later.

After winning a Victoria Cross officers, in particular, tended to reach heights in their military careers which without a Victoria Cross would have been beyond their reach. Some of these officers, promoted beyond their competence are more remembered for their incompetence than for winning the Victoria Cross. This is certainly the case of Lieutenant Colonel Redvers Henry Buller of the 60th Rifles who won his Cross at Inhlobana in March 1879, during the Zulu War. From being a very able Infantry Colonel he was quickly promoted so much so that by the time of the war in South Africa in 1899 was a General. After the many disasters of what became known as "Black Week" in December 1899 he soon became known as Sir Reverse Buller to the men in the ranks.

Throughout the years there have been many and varied forms of commemoration to recipients of the decoration. Apart from the early literature which sung the praise of Queen Victoria's Victoria Cross heroes the earliest would seem to be that nineteenth century novelty, the cigarette card. The Taddy's Cigarette Company produced a series of one hundred and twenty five cards which depicted winners from the Crimean War to the end of the century. Part of the collection was entitled Victoria Cross winners of the Boer War and amongst those shown was Edinburgh born Private Charles Thomas Kennedy of the 2nd Battalion of the Highland Light Infantry who won his Cross for rescuing a comrade at Dewetsdorp in South Africa on the 22 November 1900. Private Kennedy died in 1907 when he tried to stop a runaway horse and cart in Leith Walk in Edinburgh.

As the patriotic fervour which accompanied the drums of war in 1914 grew the Cigarette Companies again used cards to portray the exploits of these men who had won the country's highest decoration for gallantry in bygone wars. In a series which depicted thirty six winners on twenty five cards John Player and Sons retold the stories of some more Scots born winners. Included in the series were the stories of Balcarres born Captain Robert Lindsay, who was one of the first to be awarded the medal in the Crimea, and Dumbarton born Major William Babtie who was the first Scot to win a Victoria Cross during the Boer War.

As the battles in the trenches of France and Flanders began to unfold a new generation of winners came to be known. More Scots featured in cigarette cards including Edinburgh soldier Lieutenant Walter Brodie of the 2nd Battalion of the Highland Light Infantry and Glasgow born Captain Harry Ranken who had lost his life in winning his Cross while serving as Medical Officer of the 1st Battalion of the King's Royal Rifle Corps. Although the inclusion of cards in cigarette packets has now ceased the interest in Victoria Cross winners has continued into the 1980's when again John Player and Sons included in packets of Doncella Cigar cards which showed the acts of winners from the very first winner Midshipman Lucas in the Baltic Sea in 1854, to one of the last winners Lance Corporal Rambahadur Limbu of the 10th Gurkha Rifles who had won his medal fighting in the jungles of Borneo in 1965.

The depiction of winners of the Victoria Cross on cards was not an entirely adult phenomenon and in the 1960's manufacturers of children's sweets included cards as novelties showing Victoria Cross winners in action. Many Scots as usual featured in these cards including the much mentioned Major Babtie and Lieutenant Colonel Geoffrey Keyes who had been awarded his posthumous Victoria Cross for his part in leading the ill-fated raid on General Rommell's headquarters in the Libyan desert at Beda Littoria.

By far the most common form of memorial to winners of the Victoria Cross is to have their name on some monument which is only really acknowledged once a year when an annual ceremony to celebrate the peace of 1919 and remember the dead of two world wars is conducted around it. On these mainly granite monuments can be found the names of men and women who have paid the highest price for the defence of their country and included amongst them are the names of yet more winners of the country's highest decoration for gallantry. There is on the Promenade at Dunoon on the Clyde Coast one bearing the name of Innellan born Captain George Paton of the Grenadier Guards who apart from winning the Victoria Cross in death had previously been decorated with the Military Cross for another act of unselfish gallantry. Many churches throughout Scotland have in some prominent place a plaque which bears the names of those who have a connection with that particular church or parish and have been killed in war. The name of Sergeant John Meikle of the 4th Battalion of the Seaforth Highlanders who apart from the fact that he is a winner of the Victoria Cross appears on several memorials throughout the country. His name can be found in the Rolls of Honour in the Pollokshaws Methodist Church in Glasgow and in the United Free Church at Nitshill, where he was employed as a railway clerk at the railway station before he joined the Army. His name also appears on the Scottish National War Memorial in Edinburgh and was also on the Roll of Honour in the former railway station at St. Enoch's Square in Glasgow, as he was one of the many thousands of railway workers who answered the Country's call and never returned to continue with their pre war occupations.

From the 1960's through to the 1980's the newspaper group D C Thomson provided for the young a vehicle through which the stories of those men who had won the Victoria Cross could be relayed to the post Second World War generation. However those who were sufficiently interested could still meet the men who wore the ribbon of the Victoria Cross. Youngsters (usually boys) could have a weekly order with their local newsagent for the Victor Comic which featured almost every week the story told in pictures on the front and back pages of the magazine how some of the winners of the Victoria Cross had won their medals. Issue number 132 of 31 August 1963 under the heading of "Rescue from no-man's land" told of the deeds of West Lothian born Lance Corporal William Angus of the 8th Battalion the Highland Light Infantry. The brave Scot who had played for Glasgow Celtic Football Club left the relative safety of his trench near Givenchy in France to rescue a wounded officer knowing that there was no chance that he would succeed without being at least wounded. In the event he received over 40 wounds some of which were indeed very serious. Another well known winner of the Victoria Cross was honoured in the comic by having his story told on more than one occasion. Issues 654 and 836 both told the story of how Acting Flight Lieutenant William Reid from Baillieston near Glasgow had in spite of multiple injuries pressed home with his attack and only after he had completed his bombing mission did he then contemplate flying his crippled Lancaster Bomber back to his base safely.

The Victor comic of 15 May 1976 also featured a Scots born winner. His story was one of three men who had won Victoria Crosses and all had belonged to the same street in Winnipeg, Canada. The three men were Company Sergeant Major Frederick Hall of the 8th Manitoba Regiment who had won a posthumous Victoria Cross in June 1915, Acting Corporal Leo Clark of the 2nd Eastern Ontario Regiment who had won his Cross in September 1916 only to be killed in action a month later, and the final member of the trio was Ayrshire born Robert Shankland of the 43rd Battalion of the Manitoba Regiment who won his medal at Passchendaele in October 1917. The Scot was the only one of the three heroes to survive the war and was able to be present in 1925 at the renaming ceremony when a bronze plaque was placed on a lamp post in Valour Road, Winnipeg previously known as Pine Street when the three heroes went to war.

Over the years other more bizarre memorials have appeared to help people remember Victoria Cross winners amongst these have been 3 Patriot Class Railway Locomotives named after 3 employees of the London and North Western Railway Company who had won the Victoria Cross in the First World War. These were Lance Corporal John A Christie, 1/11th Battalion of the London Regiment, Private Ernest Sykes, 27th (Service) Battalion of the Northumberland Fusiliers and Private Wilfred Wood of the 10th Battalion of the Northumberland Fusiliers.

Another form of memorial was to have army barracks or even wards in military hospitals named after them. Driver Fred Luke who won his medal for saving guns which had been left behind during the retreat from Mons in 1914 had both a room in Woolwich Barracks named after him and a tank christened with his name. The Royal Air Force has honoured some of its winners by having aircraft named after them. One of the last Dakota Aircraft used by the Air Force is named after Flight Lieutenant D S A Lord who won a posthumous Victoria Cross in September 1944 during the Battle of Arnhem. In the 1960's Kenya Airlines took delivery of ten VC 10 passenger aircraft and named them after winners of the medal. Amongst the ten winners who were invited to the ceremony were Commander A C C Miers and Flight Lieutenant William Reid.

The most recent reminder about the Victoria Cross came on 11 September 1990 when 5 stamps designed by John Gibbs and illustrated by John Harwood were issued depicting the 8 major British awards for gallantry, including the highest award possible.

In the Scottish Infantry Regiments music plays an important part in the day to day running of them. Much of the history and tradition is kept alive in the music of the regimental bands. Although many tunes commemorate battles in which Victoria Crosses were won, e.g. Magersfontein and Wadi Akarit, other tunes are dedicated to officers who have brought distinction to regiments, like Brigadier Lorne Campbell of the Argyll and Sutherland Highlanders and Captain Ernest Towse, the Blind VC, of the Gordon Highlanders. However it is unusual to have ordinary soldiers honoured, in the Black Watch one of the companies has a pipe tune called "Lawson's Men" and this commemorates the exploits of two privates, Walter Cook and Duncan Millar who won Crosses at the attack on the Maylah Ghat in India in January 1859.

Of the 158 Scots born winners of the Victoria Cross just over half of them have a memorial stone or plaque in some place with which they have had a connection in life or more occasionally in death. One of the furthest away examples of this is the grave of Sergeant Samuel McGaw, from Kirkmichael in Ayrshire, of the Black Watch who after having won his Victoria Cross in the Ashanti campaign in West Africa in 1874 only to die in 1878 of heat apoplexy (heat stroke) whilst on march in the extreme heat of the Cyprus sun. He was finally laid to rest in the English cemetery in Kyrenia in the Turkish occupied area of modern Cyprus.

Although these aids to the memory of all these men who have won the nations highest award for gallantry have through the years taken on many forms, people of todays generations are for the most part incapable of remembering any of their names. They like old soldiers have not only died for their country but have faded away to be forgotten as ever having won the Victoria Cross and being immortalised in history for those deeds which over the years have helped Britain retain the Great in the eyes of the rest of the World.

APPENDIX 1

SCOTTISH BORN WINNERS LISTED ALPHABETICALLY

AIKMAN, Frederick Robertson
AITKEN, Robert Hope Moncrieff
ANDERSON, William
ANDERSON, William Herbert
ANGUS, William
ARCHIBALD, Adam
BABTIE, William *(fig.37)*
BARRON, Colin Fraser
BEACH, Thomas
BISSETT, William Davidson
BLAIR, Robert
BLOOMFIELD, William Anderson
BOGLE, Andrew Cathcart
BOUGHEY, Stanley Henry Parry
BRODIE, Walter Lorrain *(fig.35)*
BROOKE, James Anson Otho
BRUCE, William Arthur MacCrae
BUCHAN, John Crawford *(fig.13)*
CADELL, Thomas
CALDWELL, Thomas
CAMERON, Donald *(fig.25)*
CAMPBELL, John Charles *(fig.21)*
CAMPBELL, Kenneth *(figs.19,34)*
CAMPBELL, Lorne MacLaine *(fig.24)*
CARMICHAEL, John
CLAMP, William
COCHRANE, Hugh Stewart
COMBE, Robert Grierson
COOK, John
CRAIG, James
CRAIG, John Manson
CRUIKSHANK, John Alexander
  (figs.27, 42)
CUNINGHAME, William James
  Montgomery
CUNYNGHAM, William Henry
  DICK
DAVIS, James
DAWSON, James Lennox
DAYKINS, John Brunton
DOWNIE, Robert
DUNDAS, James
DUNSIRE, Robert *(fig.10)*
EDWARDS, Alexander
ERSKINE, John
EVANS, Samuel
FARMER, Donald Dickson
FARQUHARSON, Francis Edward
  Henry
FINDLATER, George *(fig.38)*
FINDLAY, George de Cardonnel
  Elmsell
FINLAY, David
FRICKLETON, Samuel *(fig.11)*
GARDNER, William
GORDON, William Eagleson

GRANT, Charles James William
  (fig.33)
GRIEVE, John
HAMILTON, John Brown
HAMILTON, Thomas de Courcy
HANNAH, John *(fig.18)*
HENDERSON, Arthur
HENDERSON, George Stuart
HENDERSON, Herbert Stephen
HOME, Anthony Dickson
HOPE, William
HUFFAM, James Palmer
HUNTER, David Ferguson
JARVIS, Charles Alfred
JOHNSTON, William Henry
JONES, Robert James Thomas
  DIGBY
KENNEDY, Charles Thomas
KENNEDY, William Hew CLARK
KER, Allan Ebenezer
KERR, William Alexander
KEYES, Geoffrey Charles Tasker
  (fig.20)
KINROSS, Cecil John
KNOX, John Simpson
LAIDLAW, Daniel
LAUDER, David Ross *(fig.36)*
LEITCH, Peter
LEITH, James
LINDSAY, Robert James *(fig.32)*
LUMLEY, Charles
McAULAY, John
McBEAN, William *(fig.4)*
McBEATH, Robert
McDERMOND, John
MacDONALD, Henry
McDOUGALL, John
McGAW, Samuel *(fig.6)*
McGREGOR, David Stuart
MacGREGOR, John
McGREGOR, Roderick
McGUFFIE, Louis *(fig.17)*
McINNES, Hugh
McINTOSH, George Imlach
MacINTYRE, David Lowe *(fig.16)*
MacINTYRE, Donald
McIVER, Hugh *(fig.15)*
MacKAY, David
MacKAY, John Frederick
McKECHNIE, James
McKENZIE, Hugh
MacKENZIE, James
MacKENZIE, John
MACKINTOSH, Donald
McNEILL, John Carstairs *(fig.5)*
MacPHERSON, Herbert Taylor

McPHERSON, Stewart
McPHIE, James
MALCOLM, Hugh Gordon *(fig.23)*
MALCOLMSON, John Grant *(fig.1)*
MAY, Henry *(fig.7)*
MEIKLE, John *(fig.14)*
MELVIN, Charles *(fig.9)*
MIERS, Anthony Cecil Capel *(fig.22)*
MILLAR, Duncan
MILLER, James
MILNE, William Johnstone
MUNRO, James
O'NEILL, John
PARK, James
PATON, George Henry Tatham
PATON, John *(fig.3)*
PERIE, John
POLLOCK, James Dalgliesh
RAMAGE, Henry
RANKEN, Harry Sherwood
REID, William *(figs.26,42)*
RENNIE, William *(fig.2)*
REYNOLDS, William
RICHARDSON, James Cleland
RIPLEY, John
RITCHIE, Henry Peel *(fig.8)*
RITCHIE, Walter Potter
ROBERTSON, William
RODGERS, George
ROSS, John
SAMSON, George McKenzie
SELLAR, George
SHANKLAND, Robert *(fig.40)*
SHAW, Same(John)
SIMPSON, John
SKINNER, John *(fig.12)*
SMITH, Archibald Bissett
SPENCE, David
SPENCE, Edward
STEWART, William George
  Drummond
STOKES, James *(fig.29)*
STRACHAN, Harcus
TAIT, James Edward
THOMPSON, Alexander
THOMPSON, George *(fig.28)*
TOLLERTON, Ross
TURNBULL, James Yuill
VOUSDEN, William John
WALLACE, Samuel Thomas Dickson
WATT, Joseph
WILSON, George
WOOD, John Augustus
YOUNG, William
YOUNGER, David Reginald

APPENDIX 2

SCOTTISH BORN WINNERS BY REGIMENT OR SERVICE

	PLACE/YEAR	TOWN/COUNTY	OTHER AWARDS	REMARKS

2nd DRAGOON GUARDS (QUEEN'S BAYS)[1st QUEEN'S DRAGOON GUARDS]

	PLACE/YEAR	TOWN/COUNTY	OTHER AWARDS	REMARKS
Lieutenant Robert Blair	India/1857	Linlithgow		

2nd DRAGOONS (ROYAL SCOTS GREYS) [ROYAL SCOTS DRAGOON GUARDS]

	PLACE/YEAR	TOWN/COUNTY	OTHER AWARDS	REMARKS
Sergeant Major John Grieve	Crimea/1854	Musselburgh		
Sergeant Henry Ramage	Crimea/1854	Edinburgh		
T/Lt.Colonel Geoffrey Keyes	N.Africa/1941	Aberdour`	MC	Attd.11th Scottish Commando

9th (QUEEN'S ROYAL) LANCERS[9th/12th ROYAL LANCERS{PRINCE OF WALES'S OWN}]

	PLACE/YEAR	TOWN/COUNTY	OTHER AWARDS	REMARKS
Troop Sergeant Major David Spence	India/1858	Inverkeithing		

14th LIGHT DRAGOONS(14th/20th {KING'S} HUSSARS)

	PLACE/YEAR	TOWN/COUNTY	OTHER AWARDS	REMARKS
Lieutenant James Leith	India/1858	Glenkindie		

ROYAL FIELD ARTILLERY (ROYAL ARTILLERY)

	PLACE/YEAR	TOWN/COUNTY	OTHER AWARDS	REMARKS
T/Lieutenant Samuel T D Wallace	France/1917	Thornhill		63rd.Brigade
A/Brigadier John C Campbell	N.Africa/1941	Thurso`	DSO(bar)MC	Commd. 7th Armoured Div.

ROYAL ENGINEERS

	PLACE/YEAR	TOWN/COUNTY	OTHER AWARDS	REMARKS
Colour Sergeant Henry MacDonald	Crimea/1855	Inverness		
Colour Sergeant Peter Leitch	Crimea/1855	Kinross	Legion D'Honneur	
Sapper John Perie	Crimea/1855	Huntly	Medaille Militaire	
Corporal John Ross	Crimea/1855	Stranraer		
Lieutenant Robert T Digby-Jones	S.Africa/1900	Edinburgh		
Lance Corporal Charles A Jarvis	Belgium/1914	Fraserburgh		57th Field Company
Captain William H Johnston	France/1914	Leith		59th Field Company
Corporal James L Dawson	France/1915	Tillicoultry		187th Company
Corporal James McPhie	France/1918	Edinburgh		416th Field Company
Sapper Adam Archibald	France/1918	Leith		218th Field Company
A/Major George D E Findlay	France/1918	Balloch	MC(bar)	409th Field Company

ROYAL ARMY MEDICAL CORPS

	PLACE/YEAR	TOWN/COUNTY	OTHER AWARDS	REMARKS
Major William Babtie	S.Africa/1899	Dumbarton	KCB,KCMG	Later Sir William
Captain Harry S Ranken	France/1914	Glasgow		Attd. 1st KRRC

GRENADIER GUARDS

	PLACE/YEAR	TOWN/COUNTY	OTHER AWARDS	REMARKS
A/Captain George H T Paton	France/1917	Innellan	MC	4th Bn.

SCOTS FUSILIER GUARDS (SCOTS GUARDS)

	PLACE/YEAR	TOWN/COUNTY	OTHER AWARDS	REMARKS
Sergeant John S Knox	Crimea/1854	Glasgow	Legion D'Honneur	Also served in Rifle Brigade
Captain Robert J Lindsay	Crimea/1854	Balcarres	KCB, Legion D'Honneur	Later Lord Wantage
Sergeant James McKechnie	Crimea/1854	Paisley		
Private William Reynolds	Crimea/1854	Edinburgh	Legion D'Honneur	
Colour Sergeant James Craig	Crimea/1855	Perth		Later served in Military Train
Private James MacKenzie	France/1914	New Abbey		2nd Bn
Sergeant John MacAulay	France/1917	Kinghorn	DCM	1st Bn

1st FOOT (THE ROYAL SCOTS)[THE ROYAL REGIMENT]

	PLACE/YEAR	TOWN/COUNTY	OTHER AWARDS	REMARKS
Private Robert Dunsire	France/1915	Buckhaven		13th Bn
Private Hugh McIver	France/1918	Linwood	MM(bar)	2nd Bn
Lieutenant David S McGregor	Belgium/1918	Edinburgh		6th Bn attd.29th Bn MGC

7th FOOT (THE ROYAL REGIMENT OF FUSILIERS)

	PLACE/YEAR	TOWN/COUNTY	OTHER AWARDS	REMARKS
Lieutenant William Hope	Crimea/1855	Edinburgh		

19th FOOT (YORKSHIRE REGIMENT)[THE GREEN HOWARDS{ALEXANDRA PRINCESS OF WALES'S OWN YORKSHIRE REGIMENT}]

	PLACE/YEAR	TOWN/COUNTY	OTHER AWARDS	REMARKS
Private Samuel Evans	Crimea/1855	Paisley		
Corporal William Anderson	France/1915	Elgin		2nd Bn
Corporal William Clamp	Belgium/1917	Motherwell		6th Bn

21st FOOT (ROYAL SCOTS FUSILIERS)[THE ROYAL HIGHLAND FUSILIERS[PRINCESS MARGARET'S OWN GLASGOW & AYRSHIRE REGIMENT]

	PLACE/YEAR	TOWN/COUNTY	OTHER AWARDS	REMARKS
Private David R Lauder	Gallipoli/1915	Airdrie	Serbian Medal for Bravery	1/4th Bn
2nd Lieutenant John M Craig	Egypt/1917	Comrie		1/4th Bn attd.1/5th Bn
2nd Lieutenant Stanley H P Boughey	Palestine/1917	Ayrshire		1/4th Bn
Sergeant Thomas Caldwell	Belgium/1918	Carluke		12th Bn

	PLACE/YEAR	TOWN/COUNTY	OTHER AWARDS	REMARKS
25th FOOT (THE KING'S OWN SCOTTISH BORDERERS)				
Piper Daniel Laidlaw	France/1915	Little Swinton		7th Bn
A/Company Sergeant Major John Skinner	Belgium/1917	Glasgow	DCM	1st Bn
A/Sergeant Louis McGuffie	Belgium/1918	Wigtown		1/5th Bn
26th & 90th FOOT (CAMERONIANS)[SCOTTISH RIFLES]				
Lieutenant William Rennie	India/1857	Elgin		
Surgeon Anthony D Home	India/1857	Dunbar	KCB	Later Sir Anthony
Private Henry May	France/1914	Glasgow		1st Bn
Sergeant John Erskine	France/1916	Dunfermline		5th Bn
30th & 59th FOOT (THE EAST LANCASHIRE REGIMENT)[THE QUEEN'S LANCASHIRE REGIMENT]				
Private William Young	France/1915	Glasgow		8th(S)Bn
33rd & 76th FOOT(THE DUKE OF WELLINGTON'S[WEST RIDING] REGIMENT)				
2nd Lieutenant James Huffam	France/1918	Dunblane		5th Bn attd.2nd Bn
34th & 55th FOOT (THE BORDER REGIMENT)[THE KING'S OWN ROYAL BORDER REGIMENT]				
Private Thomas Beach	Crimea/1854	Dundee		
35th & 107th FOOT (THE ROYAL SUSSEX REGIMENT)[THE QUEEN'S REGIMENT]				
Lieutenant Colonel John C McNeill	New Zealand/1864	Colonsay	KCVO,KCB,KCMG	Later Sir John
42nd & 73rd FOOT (THE BLACK WATCH)[ROYAL HIGHLAND REGIMENT]				
Lieutenant Francis E H Farquharson	India/1858	Glasgow		
Private Edward Spence	India/1858	Dumfries		Earliest posthumous award
Private James Davis	India/1858	Edinburgh		
Quartermaster Sergeant John Simpson	India/1858	Edinburgh		
Lance Corporal Alexander Thompson	India/1858	Edinburgh		
Colour Sergeant William Gardner	India/1858	Nemphlar	MSM	
Private Duncan Millar	India/1859	Kilmarnock		
Lance Sergeant Samuel McGaw	Ashanti/1874	Kirkmichael		
Corporal John Ripley	France/1915	Keith		1st Bn
Lance Corporal David Finlay	France/1915	Guardbridge		2nd Bn
Private Charles Melvin	Mesopotamia/1917	Montrose		2nd Bn
44th & 56th FOOT (THE ESSEX REGIMENT)[THE ROYAL ANGLIAN REGIMENT]				
Private John McDougall	China/1860	Edinburgh		
47th & 81st FOOT (THE LOYAL NORTH LANCASHIRE REGIMENT)[THE QUEEN'S LANCASHIRE REGIMENT]				
Private John McDermond	Crimea/1854	Clackmannan		
53rd & 85th FOOT (THE KING'S SHROPSHIRE LIGHT INFANTRY)[THE LIGHT INFANTRY]				
Private James Stokes	Germany/1945	Glasgow		2nd Bn
63rd & 96th FOOT (MANCHESTER REGIMENT)[THE KING'S REGIMENT]				
Captain George S Henderson	Mesopotamia/1920	East Gordon	DSO(bar)MC	2nd Bn
64th & 98th FOOT (PRINCE OF WALES'S NORTH STAFFORDSHIRE REGIMENT)[THE STAFFORDSHIRE REGIMENT]				
Sergeant John Carmichael	Belgium/1917	Airdrie	MM	9th Bn
65th & 84th FOOT (THE YORK & LANCASTER REGIMENT)				
A/Sergeant John B Daykins	France/1918	Ormiston		2/4th Bn
68th & 106th FOOT (DURHAM LIGHT INFANTRY)[THE LIGHT INFANTRY]				
Captain Thomas D Hamilton	Crimea/1855	Stranraer	Legion D'Honneur	
71st & 74th FOOT(HIGHLAND LIGHT INFANTRY)[ROYAL HIGHLAND FUSILIERS][PRINCESS MARGARET'S OWN GLASGOW & AYRSHIRE REGIMENT]				
Private George Rodgers	India/1858	Glasgow		
Private Charles T Kennedy	S.Africa/1900	Edinburgh		2nd Bn
Private George Wilson	France/1914	Edinburgh		2nd Bn
Captain Walter L Brodie	Belgium/1914	Edinburgh	MC	2nd Bn
Lance Corporal William Angus	France/1915	Armadale		8th Bn
Sergeant James Y Turnbull	France/1916	Glasgow		17th Bn
A/Lance Corporal John B Hamilton	Belgium/1917	Dumbarton		1/9th Bn
A/Lieutenant Colonel William H Anderson	France/1918	Glasgow		12th(S)Bn, Commanded 12th(S)Bn
Corporal David Hunter	France/1918	Dunfermline		1/5th Bn

72nd & 78th FOOT (SEAFORTH HIGHLANDERS)[QUEEN'S OWN HIGHLANDERS]{SEAFORTH & CAMERONS}

	PLACE/YEAR	TOWN/COUNTY	OTHER AWARDS	REMARKS
Lieutenant Andrew C Bogle	India/1857	Glasgow		
Lieutenant Herbert T MacPherson	India/1857	Ardersier	KCB,KCSI	
Colour Sergeant Stewart McPherson	India/1857	Culross		
Lance Corporal George Sellar	Afghanistan/1879	Keith		
Sergeant John MacKenzie	Ashanti/1900	Contin		Attd. West African Field Force
Drummer Walter P Ritchie	France/1916	Glasgow		2nd Bn
Lieutenant Donald MacKintosh	France/1916	Glasgow		3rd Bn
Sergeant Alexander Edwards	Belgium/1917	Lossiemouth		1/6th Bn
Lance Corporal Robert McBeath	France/1917	Kinlochbervie		1/5th Bn
Sergeant John Meikle	France/1918	Kirkintilloch	MM	4th Bn

75th & 92nd FOOT (THE GORDON HIGHLANDERS)

Lieutenant William H Dick-Cunyngham	Afghanistan/1879	Edinburgh		
Piper George Findlater	India/1897	Forgue		1st Bn
Sergeant Major William Robertson	S.Africa/1899	Dumfries	CBE, Legion D'Honneur	2nd Bn
Lance Corporal John F MacKay	S.Africa/1900	Edinburgh		1st Bn
Captain David R Younger	S.Africa/1900	Edinburgh		1st Bn
Captain William E Gordon	S.Africa/1900	Bridge of Allan	CBE	1st Bn
Lieutenant James A O Brooke	Belgium/1914	Aberdeen		2nd Bn
Private George I McIntosh	Belgium/1917	Buckie		1/6th Bn
Lieutenant Allan E Ker	France/1918	Edinburgh		3rd Bn attd. 61st Bn MGC

79th FOOT (QUEEN'S OWN CAMERON HIGHLANDERS){QUEEN'S OWN HIGHLANDERS}[SEAFORTH & CAMERONS]

Sergeant Donald Farmer	S.Africa/1900	Kelso	MSM	1st Bn
Private Ross Tollerton	France/1914	Hurlford		1st Bn
Corporal James D Pollock	France/1915	Tillicoultry		5th Bn

83rd & 86th FOOT (ROYAL IRISH RIFLES){THE ROYAL IRISH RANGERS}

Lieutenant Hugh Cochrane	India/1858	Fort William		

91st & 93rd FOOT (THE ARGYLL & SUTHERLAND HIGHLANDERS)

Private David MacKay	India/1857	Thurso		
Colour Sergeant James Munro	India/1857	Nigg		
Sergeant John Paton	India/1857	Stirling		
Captain William G D Stewart	India/1857	Grandtully		
Lieutenant William McBean	India/1858	Inverness		Held every rank, Private to Major General
A/Captain Arthur Henderson	France/1917	Paisley	MC	4th Bn attd.2nd Bn
2nd Lieutenant John C Buchan	France/1918	Alloa		7th Bn attd.8th Bn
T/Lieutenant David L MacIntyre	France/1918	Portnahaven	CB	Attd.1/6th Bn Highland Light Infantry
Lieutenant William D Bissett	France/1918	St. Martins	Croix de Guerre	1/6th Bn
T/Lieutenant Colonel Lorne M Campbell	N.Africa/1943	Argyllshire	DSO(bar)TD	Commanded 7th Bn

97th FOOT (ROYAL WEST KENT REGIMENT)[THE QUEEN'S REGIMENT]

Captain Charles Lumley	Crimea/1855	Forres	Legion D'Honneur	

100th & 109th FOOT (PRINCE OF WALES'S LEINSTER REGIMENT)[ROYAL CANADIANS]

Sergeant John O'Neill	Belgium/1918	Airdrie	MM, Medaille Militaire	2nd Bn

102nd & 103rd FOOT (THE ROYAL DUBLIN FUSILIERS)

Sergeant Robert Downie	France/1916	Glasgow	MM	2nd Bn

THE RIFLE BRIGADE (THE PRINCE CONSORTS OWN)[THE ROYAL GREEN JACKETS]

Lieutenant William J M Cuninghame	Crimea/1854	Ayr		1st Bn, MP for Ayr 1874'80
Private Roderick McGregor	Crimea/1855	Inverness		2nd Bn
Private John Shaw	India/1858	Prestonpans	DCM	3rd Bn

ROYAL NAVY

Commander Henry P Ritchie	E.Africa	Edinburgh		
Commander Anthony C C Miers	Corfu/1942	Inverness	KBE,CB,DSO(bar)Legion of Merit(USA)	

ROYAL NAVY RESERVE

Seaman George M Samson	Gallipoli/1915	Carnoustie		
T/Lieutenant Archibald B Smith	Atlantic/1917	Cults		
Skipper Joseph Watt	Straits of Otranto/1917	Gardenstown	Croix de Guerre, Italian Military Medal	
Lieutenant Donald Cameron	Norway/1943	Carluke		

ROYAL AIR FORCE

Sergeant John Hannah	Belgium/1940	Paisley		83 Squadron
Wing Commander Hugh G Malcolm	N.Africa/1942	Broughty Ferry		18 Squadron

ROYAL AIR FORCE VOLUNTEER RESERVE

Flying Officer Kenneth Campbell	France/1941	Saltcoats		22 Squadron
A/Flight Lieutenant William Reid	Germany/1943	Baillieston		61 Squadron
Flying Officer John A Cruickshank	At Sea/1944	Aberdeen		210 Squadron (Coastal Command)
Flight Sergeant George Thompson	Germany/1945	Trinity Gask		9 Squadron

	PLACE/YEAR	TOWN/COUNTY	OTHER AWARDS	REMARKS
		INDIAN ARMY		
2ND BENGAL FUSILIERS				
Lieutenant Thomas Cadell	India/1857	Cockenzie	CB	
3rd BOMBAY LIGHT CAVALRY				
Lieutenant John G Malcolmson	Persia/1857	Inverness	MVO	
4th BENGAL NATIVE INFANTRY				
Lieutenant Frederick R Aikman	India/1858	Lanarkshire		
13th BENGAL NATIVE INFANTRY				
Lieutenant Robert H M Aitken	India/1857	Cupar	CB	
20th BOMBAY NATIVE INFANTRY				
Captain James A Wood	Persia/1856	Fort William		
24th BOMBAY NATIVE INFANTRY				
Lieutenant William A Kerr	India/1857	Melrose		
BENGAL STAFF CORPS				
Major Donald MacIntyre	India/1872	Kincraig		Attd.2nd Gurkha Rifles
Captain John Cook	Afghanistan/1878	Edinburgh		Attd.5th Gurkha Rifles
Captain William J Vousden	Afghanistan/1879	Perth	CB	Attd.5th Punjab Cavalry
BENGAL ENGINEERS				
Lieutenant James Dundas	India/1865	Edinburgh		
BENGAL ARTILLERY				
Gunner James Park	India/1857	Glasgow		
Gunner Hugh MacInnes	India/1857	Glasgow		
BENGAL ORDNANCE DEPARTMENT				
Conductor James Miller	India/1857	Glasgow		
INDIAN STAFF CORPS				
Lieutenant Charles J W Grant	Burma/1891	Bourtie		
59th SCINDE RIFLES				
Lieutenant William A M Bruce	France/1914	Edinburgh		
		SOUTH AFRICAN ARMY		
BULAWAYO FIELD FORCE				
Trooper Herbert S Henderson	Rhodesia/1896	Glasgow		
SCOUT CORPS				
Captain William A Bloomfield	E.Africa/1916	Edinburgh		Attd.2nd S.African Mounted Brigade
		CANADIAN ARMY		
CANADIAN MACHINE GUN CORPS				
Lieutenant Hugh MacKenzie	Belgium/1917	Inverness	DCM, Croix de Guerre	7th Company
ALBERTA REGIMENT				
Private Cecil Kinross	Belgium/1917	Clackmannan		49th Bn
CENTRAL ONTARIO REGIMENT				
Corporal Colin F Barron	Belgium/1917	Boyndie		3rd Bn
T/Captain John MacGregor	France/1918	Cawdor	MC(bar),DCM ,ED	1st Bn attd.2nd Canadian Mounted Rifles
FORT GARRY HORSE				
Lieutenant Harcus Strachan	France/1917	Bo'ness	MC	
MANITOBA REGIMENT				
Piper James C Richardson	France/1916	Bellshill		16th Bn Canadian Scottish
Private William J Milne	France/1917	Wishaw		16th Bn Canadian Scottish
Lieutenant Robert G Combe	France/1917	Aberdeen		27th Bn
Lieutenant Robert Shankland	Belgium/1917	St. Quivox	DCM	43rd Bn
Lieutenant James E Tait	France/1918	Dumfries	MC	78th Bn Winnipeg Grenadiers
QUEBEC REGIMENT				
Lieutenant Colonel William H Clark-Kennedy	France/1918	Dunskey	CMG,DSO(bar)Croix de Guerre 03	24th Bn Victoria Rifles
		NEW ZEALAND ARMY		
NEW ZEALAND RIFLE BRIGADE				
Lance Corporal Samuel Frickleton	Belgium/1917	Slamannan		3rd Bn

APPENDIX 3

WINNERS WITH CLOSE SCOTTISH ASSOCIATION

Although the scope of this book has been as an aide memoir for all those winners of the Victoria Cross who were born in Scotland, there are many winners who considered themselves as Scottish but who by an accident of birth place are not featured in the previous pages.

The British and Indian Armies in Queen Victoria's time was peppered with officers from Scotland and many of these officers had their wives in the country in which they were serving. This of course meant that any children born abroad could claim to be Scottish without actually having been born in the country.

In the action at Nawa Kili, in the upper Swat Valley in India on the 17th August 1897 three men won Victoria Crosses for their efforts to rescue an officer of the Lancashire Fusiliers who was severely wounded and was lying exposed to the attention of native swordsmen. In the action one of the officers was shot and killed and was not confirmed as winning a Victoria Cross until the London Gazette of the 15th January 1907 confirmed that King Edward VII himself had sanctioned the award to Lieutenant Hector MacLean of the Corps of Guides. The awards to the other two officers Lieutenant Robert Adams and Viscount Alexander Fincastle were announced in the Gazette of the 9th November 1897. All three men had strong Scottish connections. Although he was born in a tent at Bannu in the North-west Frontier Hector MacLean was the son of Major General Charles MacLean and Margaret Bairnsfather of Dumbarrow in Forfarshire, and was educated at Edinburgh and St. Andrews. Lieutenant Adams served throughout his career in the Indian Army and retired to Inverness where he died on 13th February 1928. He was cremated in Glasgow a few days later. The third winner Viscount Fincastle was the son of Lord Dunmore who had estates in Scotland. Although he was born in London he eventually became the 8th Earl of Dunmore on the death of his father in 1907. In 1904 he married Lucinda the daughter of Colonel Kemble of Knock Farm in the Isle of Skye.

The numbers of winners in the First World War included more who had strong Scottish connections and amongst them was Lance Corporal John Alexander Christie who won his Cross for bravery at Fejja in Palestine on 21/22 December 1917 when he cleared an enemy communication trench by his prompt action and as a result saved many lives. Jock Christie as he was known was born in London, the son of Scottish parents and went on to be the first Treasurer of the Victoria Cross Association when it was formed in 1956.

Another winner with Scottish connections was Brigadier General John Vaughan Campbell who won his Cross while serving with the Coldstream Guards at Guinchy in France on 15th September 1916. General Campbell was a great uncle of the Earl of Cawdor, who died in 1993, and when he himself died in 1944 his ashes were scattered over the Cawdor Estate in Nairnshire in Scotland. Another winner from the First World War who was not born in Scotland but came from Scottish parents was Lieutenant John Graham who was awarded the Victoria Cross for gallantry in Mesopotamia for good work with his machine guns while serving with the Machine Gun Corps. Lieutenant Colonel Graham became the 3 Baron Larbert and took over the estates on Loch Lomond when his father the second Baron died in 1936. He died in Edinburgh on 6th December 1980.

On of the first winners of the Victoria Cross in 1914 was Driver Fred Luke of the Royal Field Artillery who won his decoration during the retreat from Mons by helping to save the guns at Le Cateau. Fred Luke returned to Britain after serving throughout the war and married Jeannie Husband and went to live in Glasgow. He was the one winner which I used to see on a fairly regular basis and in his later life was always described in the press as one of Scotland's quiet Victoria Cross winners.

The return to world hostilities in 1939 added even more names to the roll of Victoria Cross winners and a few more who although Scottish were not born in Scotland.

As the war in North Africa was coming to an end The Lord Lyell a Captain in the Scots Guards won his Cross for outstanding leadership and gallantry over the period from the 22nd of April 1943 until his death on the 27th April at Dj Bou Arada in Tunisia. The announcement of the Victoria Cross for the Lord Lyell in the Victoria Cross confirmed that he lived in Kirriemuir in Scotland. He was the only son of Lord Lyell.

Another Second World War winner who lived in Kirriemuir was Richard Burton who won his Cross at Monte Ceco in Italy in October 1944 when he took on a Spandau machine gun position and captured it after killing three of the crew. After the war ended he went to live in the town where sadly he died in July 1993.

There is no doubt that there are many winners of the country's highest award for gallantry in the face of an enemy who have some kind of Scottish connection because Scottish soldiers have left a legacy of heroism throughout the world and are still to be seen and heard in the battlefields of todays high-tech wars.

BIBLIOGRAPHY

FOR VALOUR; Ian S Uys

VC's OF THE AIR; John F Turner

VC's OF THE NAVY; John F Turner

BRITAIN'S ROLL OF GLORY; D H Parry

VC's OF WALES & THE WELSH REGIMENT; W Alister Williams

THE STORY OF THE VICTORIA CROSS; Brig. The Rt. Hon. J Smyth VC MC MP

BRAVE RAILWAYMEN; Allan Stanistreet

THE REGISTER OF THE VICTORIA CROSS; This England Books

VALIANT MEN; Edited by John Swettenham

THE VICTORIA CROSS; Centenary Book 1956

THE BOYS BOOK OF VC HEROES; Newton Branch

FOR VALOUR; Thames Television

THE BRONZE CROSS; F Gordon Roe

THE VICTORIA CROSS 1856'1920; J B Hayward & Son

VC's OF THE SOMME; Gerald Gliddon

THE FROGMEN; Waldron & Gleeson

STRIKE HARD, STRIKE SURE; Ralph Barker

BRITISH BATTLES & MEDALS; Spink

THE WAR ILLUSTRATED; Edited by Hammerton

BRITISH BATTLES ON LAND & SEA; James Grant

THE GREAT WAR WITH RUSSIA; W H Russell

THE TALE OF THE GREAT MUTINY; W H Fitchett

THE PERSONAL LIFE OF QUEEN VICTORIA; Sarah A Tooley

THE ANATOMY OF COURAGE; Lord Moran

COASTAL COMMAND; HMSO

THE HIGHLAND DIVISION; HMSO

THEY SOUGHT OUT ROMMEL; HMSO

PORTRAIT OF A SOLDIER, Dingwall Museum Trust

PRIVATE WILLIAM YOUNG VC; Henry L Kirby

SUBMARINE "TORBAY"; Paul Chapman

FORTY ONE YEARS IN INDIA; Field Marshall Lord Roberts VC

THE QUEEN'S OWN HIGHLANDERS; Lieutenant Colonel Angus Fairrie

WITH THE SCOTTISH RIFLES VOLUNTEERS AT THE FRONT; Godfrey N Smith

THE GORDON HIGHLANDERS; Christopher Sinclair-Stevenson

A SOLDIER'S HISTORY; The Royal Highland Fusiliers Museum

VC WINNERS MENTIONED IN TEXT

INDEX